AF662222

ACT EAST AND INDIA'S NORTH-EAST

Editors

C. Joshua Thomas

Konthoujam Sarda

PENTAGON PRESS

Act East and India's North-East

Editors: C. Joshua Thomas and Konthoujam Sarda

First Published in 2017

Copyright © ICSSR-NERC, Shillong

ISBN 978-81-8274-954-2

All rights reserved. No part of this publication may be reproduced, stored in a retrieval system, or transmitted, in any form or by any means, electronic, mechanical, photocopying, recording, or otherwise, without first obtaining written permission of the copyright owner.

Disclaimer: The views expressed in this book are those of the authors and do not necessarily reflect those of the editors.

Published by
PENTAGON PRESS
206, Peacock Lane, Shahpur Jat
New Delhi-110049
Phones: 011-64706243, 26491568
Telefax: 011-26490600
email: rajan@pentagonpress.in
website: www.pentagonpress.in

Printed at Avantika Printers Private Limited.

Contents

Foreword

I am delighted to present the book *Act East and India's North-East: How to Reap the Dividend*, which is an outcome of the brainstorming session held during the inauguration of the ASEAN Studies Centre in Shillong on 8th August 2016.

The ASEAN Studies Centre is a unique regional think-tank specially conceived to generate ideas on how to enhance engagement between the North-Eastern region of India and the ten South East Asian countries.

The brainstorming session was the first academic activity conducted by the ASEAN Studies Centre and was inaugurated by Shri V. Shanmuganathan, Governor of Meghalaya, in the presence of Shri S.K. Srivastava, Vice-Chancellor of the North Eastern Hill University, as well as several noted academics, opinion makers and senior diplomats, past and present.

This volume recaps the key points made and deliberated upon during the brainstorming session and captures the essence of 'Acting East through the North-East' via political, economic and socio-cultural initiatives.

I trust this publication will serve as an important thought piece on India's Act East Policy and that scholars and researchers of international relations, international trade, economics, politics and particularly those working on North-East India will find it of relevance.

Ms. Pooja Kapur
Joint Secretary (ASEAN Multilateral)
Ministry of External Affairs
Government of India, New Delhi

Inaugural Address

Shri V. Shangmuganathan
Honourable Governor of Meghalaya

Dignitaries on the dais, distinguished participants, ladies and gentlemen!

I am delighted to be present at this August gathering of the 1st Academic Session, 'Act East and India's North-East: How to Reap the Dividend', organised by the ASEAN Studies Centre, Indian Council of Social Science Research (ICSSR)-North Eastern Regional Centre (NERC), North-Eastern Hill University (NEHU), Campus, Shillong. It gives me great pleasure to know that the Centre has been inaugurated just 8(eight) months after the announcement of the proposal to open an ASEAN Studies Centre at NEHU by the Hon'ble Prime Minister of India, Shri Narendra Modiji in his opening statement at the India-ASEAN Summit in November 2015 at Kuala Lumpur. This also symbolises the importance and high priority that the Hon'ble Prime Minister attaches both, to the country's relations with the ASEAN countries as well as the pivotal role that is envisaged for the North-East India in fostering these relations further.

It is heartening to note that the Ministry of External Affairs (MEA), Government of India, has entrusted this challenging task to ICSSR-NERC, NEHU Campus. I have high expectations that the ICSSR North-Eastern Regional Centre, an autonomous research institute and a noted think-tank in the country will meaningfully participate, contribute and engage in research and dialogue in connecting the North-Eastern states of India with the ASEAN Community. With the Hon'ble Prime Minister of India, Shri Narendra Modiji making our South-East Asian neighbours, a foreign policy priority, the now re-named "Act East Policy" redraws the importance of India's North-Eastern states as the gateway to Southeast Asian countries.

India launched the Look East Policy (LEP) in the 1990s to develop close ties with the ASEAN countries. It is well known that India has had close historical links with the South East Asian Countries, particularly in the fields of commerce and culture. Ancient history has enough evidence that India had dynamic cultural and commercial engagements with South East Asia. Till the 12th Century A.D, these relations prospered on the basis of philosophical and cultural contacts. Hinduism, and later Buddhism, were the vehicles for the synthesis of a common cultural entity in the region. The popularity of Ramayana with varying nuances from one country to the other, engravings of the Mahabharata and Ramayana in the temples of Angkor Wat in Cambodia, and Luang Prabang in Laos, besides the eminence of Nalanda University, are testimony to our cultural and religious ties. These cultural relations in turn also promoted trade.

Today, ASEAN and India together represent a combined population of over 2(two) billion and a GDP of over U.S $3.8 trillion, creating one of the largest economies of the world. India-ASEAN relations have progressed steadily since the 1990s and India is now a strategic partner of the ASEAN. India and ASEAN share convergence of interest on several fronts. Both are strong economies and attractive markets. The expansion of India's relations with the region can be gauged from the fact that trade between India and ASEAN multiplied from US $3 billion in 1990 to almost US $ 80 billion now, and is expected to grow exponentially in the coming years. Beyond Trade, economic co-operation between India and ASEAN now extends, to sectors like tourism, transport and infrastructure, agriculture, forestry, human resource development, science and technology, health and pharmaceuticals, small and medium enterprises, information and communication technology and green energy. India and ASEAN relations also extend to political, security and cultural cooperation.

Experience shows that re-development of close linkages in the field of culture and higher technical education eventually leads to growth in several other areas also. In this context, given India's growing relations with South East Asia, I believe the North-Eastern region will have a huge role to play in India's "Act East Policy" given its geographic proximity to the Southeast Asian region. North-East India can serve as the cultural bridge between India and Southeast Asia.

India's Act East Policy has three basic components:

1) It has its emphasis on trade, investment and tourism to harness the human and capital potential between the two sides.
2) It aims for the promotion and development of North-Eastern states of India and aims at better and dependable transport connectivity.
3) It also aims to build bilateral and multilateral relations with Southeast Asian countries.

In a nutshell, we can say that the 'Act East Policy' has both geo-economic and geo-political objective with a desire to incorporate the development of the North-Eastern states of India.

North-East India shares borders with China, Nepal, Bhutan, Myanmar and Bangladesh culminating in a 4500-kilometre long international border. The historical trade links between the North-Eastern part of India and the Southeast Asian countries were severed during the colonial rule and the revival of connectivity and trade will enhance India-ASEAN trade. Border trade between

India (through the North-Eastern states) and ASEAN is said to have a huge potential. Potential for trade and investment includes skill development, agricultural products, manufacturing and synergy among others. North-East India stands to gain through project initiatives such as India-Myanmar Friendship Road or the Moreh-Tamu- Kalewa Road, India-Myanmar-Thailand Trilateral Highway, Kaladan Multimodal project and the Optical fibre network between North-East India and Southeast Asia. I am happy to say that North-East India is poised to benefit from India's growing relations with Southeast Asia as the process of globalisation has shown how cross-border trade ushers in prosperity for the people.

India's 'Act East through the North-East' will also assure this region of its due right to all-round development ensuring economic prosperity. I believe the people of the North-Eastern states will benefit immensely from these initiatives and this newly established ASEAN Studies Centre here at NEHU is meant to facilitate the enhancing of people-to-people contact, dialogue engagements, connectivity and so on which, I am sure you will deliberate at length during the course of this Brainstorming session. I extend my best wishes to the Study Centre with the hope that it will fulfil its mandate in the very near future. With these words, I have great pleasure in inaugurating this academic session on 'Act East and India's North-East'.

Contributors

Bhagirathi Panda is a faculty member at the department of Economics, North-Eastern Hill University, Shillong.
Email: bhagirathi2@yahoo.co.in

C. Joshua Thomas is the Coordinator, ASEAN Studies Centre & Deputy Director, Indian Council of Social Science Research, North Eastern Regional Centre, Shillong.
Email: cjoshuathomas@gmail.com

Gurudas Das is a faculty member of Economics in the Department of Humanities and Social Sciences, NIT Silchar.
Email: gurudas_das@yahoo.co.in

H. Srikanth is a faculty member at the Department of Political Science, North-Eastern Hill University, Shillong.
Email: hskant@gmail.com

Konthoujam Sarda is a Research Associate at the ASEAN Studies Centre, Shillong.
Email: sarda_kont@hotmail.com

Munmun Majumdar is a faculty member at the Department of Political Science, North-Eastern Hill University, Shillong.
Email: munmunmaj@yahoo.com

P.P. Srivastava is an IAS (Retd.) and Formerly Member of North Eastern Council & Chairman, North East Regional Education Council, Shillong.
Email: ppshri@gmail.com

Prabir De is the Coordinator of ASEAN-India Centre (AIC), New Delhi, and Professor, Research and Information System for Developing Countries (RIS), New Delhi.
Email: prabirde@hotmail.com

Sanjeeb Kakoty is a faculty member at the Indian Institute of Management, Shillong.
Email: sky@iimshillong.ac.in

Ujjwal Paul is a Research Scholar in the Department of Humanities and Social Sciences, NIT Silchar.
Email: ujjwal.paul@gmail.com

V. Suryanarayan is founding Director and former Senior Professor, Centre for South and Southeast Asian Studies, University of Madras.
Email: suryageeth@gmail.com

Vidyasagar Reddy is a faculty member at the Department of Political Science, Mizoram University, Aizawl.
Email: kalmekolanvreddy@gmail.com

W. Lawrence S. Prabhakar is a faculty member at the Department of Political Science, Madras Christian College, Chennai, India.
Email: lawrence.prabhakar@gmail.com

Introduction

The start of 1990s brought in a fresh perspective in India's outlook towards its South-East Asian neighbours. It is well known that the focus of India's Look East Policy in the first phase was to forge closer economic ties with ASEAN member states. Consequently, India became a Sectoral Dialogue Partner in March 1993, a Full Dialogue Partner in 1995, a member of the ASEAN Regional Forum in July 1996, a Summit Level Partner in 2002 and the relationship culminated into a Strategic Partnership in 2012.

The second phase, which began in 2003, is more comprehensive in its coverage, extending from Australia to East Asia, with ASEAN as its core and incorporated wider security issues. The rapid expansion of India's relations with the region can be very well gauged from the fact that the trade between India and ASEAN multiplied fourfold—from US$ 3.1 billion in 1991 to US$ 45 billion in 2010-11 and to US$ 65 billion in 2015. Further, ASEAN-India Free Trade Agreement (FTA) in Goods came into force on 1st January 2010 and the ASEAN-India FTA in Service and Investment in 2015.

In this context, considering India's growing relations with the neighbouring Southeast Asian countries, the North-Eastern Region (NER) will have a huge role to play in India's "Act East Policy" given its geographic proximity to the Southeast Asian region. The North-Eastern states shares borders with China, Nepal, Bhutan, Myanmar, and Bangladesh culminating in a 4500-km long international border. The states of Arunachal Pradesh, Manipur, Mizoram, and Nagaland share a 1643-km long land border with Myanmar. Northeast India is poised to benefit from India's growing relations with Southeast Asia as the process of globalization has shown how cross-border market access can uplift people from poverty, economic backwardness and bring in prosperity.

The historical trade links between the North-Eastern part of India and the Southeast Asian countries were severed during the colonial rule, and the revival of connectivity will enhance trade between the two regions. Border trade between India (through the North-Eastern states) and CLMV (Cambodia, Laos, Myanmar and Vietnam) countries (through Myanmar) is offer huge potential. Potential for trade and investment between India and the CLMV countries includes skill development, agricultural products, manufacturing, project exports, and energy among others. India and ASEAN connectivity projects to enhance trade include the India-Myanmar-Thailand Trilateral Highway and its extension to Lao PDR and Cambodia, and the new highway project connecting India-Myanmar-Lao PDR-Vietnam-Cambodia as well as developing the Mekong-India Economic Corridor (MIEC) connecting Southeast Asia to South Asia.

There is a need for rigorous development of India's North-East region in order to make India's Act East Policy successful. Shared cultural heritage, rich diversity of languages and traditions provide ample opportunity for close cooperation between India's North-East region and the South-East Asian neighbours. The people of the North-East India share common geographical features and natural resources with the border regions of Myanmar.

In spite of being the bridge-head, the NER could not reap any perceptible tangible benefits from India's Look East Policy. With the latest Act East edition and further deepening of India-ASEAN relations, it is imperative that this shortcoming is covered up. As the region is about to be transformed from landlocked to land linked following the execution of a number of cross-border road, railway and waterway connectivity, it is imperative to articulate as to what the region can offer to the people of neighbouring countries.

1. Where does the comparative advantage of the North-Eastern states lie?
2. What are the market signals that the states can look into while formulating their own development strategy?
3. In what ways can the cross-border affinities be utilized for economic well-being of the people in this region?
4. What is the status of sectoral development in the North-Eastern states?
5. What is the status of resource availability in the region?
6. What is the status of cross-border trade and investment in the bordering states in the region?
7. Are the resource structures of the North-Eastern states complementary to the demand structures of the neighbouring countries?
8. How can the productive processes of the region be integrated with the global value chain?

Keeping this context in mind the Ministry of External Affairs, Government of India entrusted the task of organising a Brainstorming Session on *Act East and India's North-East: How to Reap the Dividend* on the auspices of the inauguration of the ASEAN Studies Centre, Shillong on 8th August 2016. This volume captures the important issues which were deliberated during the Brainstorming Session.

Pointing out that India and ASEAN are becoming more economically integrated with ample scope for deepening this integration process, Prabir De in his article titled *Look East to Act East: India's Economic Engagements with ASEAN* points out that given India's diversity and geographical contrasts, an integrated transport network with South-East Asia in particular is required to support the integration process. He stressed upon the point that

India's growing linkages with ASEAN offer rich dividends for North-East India and in order to reap this benefit the North-Eastern states has to improve its 'backend' soft and hard infrastructure, which will not only help the region to raise its competitiveness but also narrow the development gaps. Stronger connectivity across NER will build a stronger network of cross-border production chains, particularly with Southeast Asia and Bangladesh. The development of economic corridors taking countries in the region will facilitate investments as well as spur economic growth in India's southern and NER as well as in Myanmar and the Mekong countries.

W. Lawrence S. Prabhakar in his article *Maritime Perspectives of India's Act East Policy and its Implications for India's Emerging Consensus of Engagement* analyses the growing interdependence of India and ASEAN in its comprehensive engagement and examined the impact of new regional and trans-regional economic dynamics and the emerging convergent and cooperative dimensions of security ties between India-ASEAN and India and the Asia-Pacific. In its contemporary essence, the imperative for India is to envision this civilizational and cultural "soft power" accents into the region and on to the East Pacific—in the quest for "Act East". "Act East" has thus the geo-historical, economic-commercial-trade and cultural engagements bolstered by very strong overseas Indian presence from North-East and South Peninsular India of the Coromandal coast. The Continental and Maritime corridors axes with South-East Asia has resulted in expansion of India's engagement with the Asia-Pacific (continental) and the Indo-Pacific (maritime) with its new and existing regional and trans-regional networks of organizations. India's engagement in South-East Asia has been premised on India's growing economic trade, commercial investments, economic and trade interdependence that has directed the strategic engagement with the region. India's role in the region is expanding in terms of how its presence and partnerships could shape the Asian security architecture that has important strategic implications.

Stressing upon the issues such as undefined property rights, costs of negotiation and enforcement of contracts Bhagirathi Panda in his article *Act East Policy, Transactions Costs and Development of the North-East* suggests that sub-optimal regional economic integration need to be addressed for significant reduction in transactions costs for development of trade between North-East India and ASEAN-Bangladesh-China. Presently such an 'establishment space' in development in the NER which is a combination of four establishments i.e. the government, community, market and civil society in varying degrees exhibits 'disproportionate parallelism'. Therefore, the ultimate success of the AEP in terms of dovetailing it as a strategy of development for the region depends on how quickly and efficiently we realise this convergence across these establishments.

C. Joshua Thomas in his article *Look North-East before Acting East: Synergising North-East with Act East Policy* locates NER's space in India's Act East Policy (AEP) and argues that integrating the region's economy with that of Bangladesh through better connectivity is crucial to the success of AEP.

In their article *Reaping Dividend from India's Act East Policy: What North-East can Offer?* Ujjwal Paul and Gurudas Das's highlights the trade potential of four prominent resources of the region namely pineapple, ginger, bamboo and hydropower and suggests measures to integrate these resources with the global value chain.

Giving an overview of 50 years of India-ASEAN relations, V. Suryanarayan in his article titled *Five Decades of ASEAN: An Indian Perspective* points out that 2017 will be an important milestone in the evolution of ASEAN as a regional organisation which will be completing its 50th year. During these five decades, ASEAN has faced inter-related internal and external challenges and its relations with China have undergone sharp twists and turns. He gives an Indian perspective on whether ASEAN will continue to function as a united and cohesive organisation.

H. Srikanth in his article titled *India-ASEAN Economic*

Integration Need to Address Political and Security Concerns stresses on the issue that economic development takes place only in an environment of mutual trust, friendship and understanding between the nations. He points out that if this is not handled properly, the security problems within and between the nations can mar the economic prospects. Similarly, immature political handling of the internal and external contradictions will hinder the attempts at economic integration. As long as the Act East Policy remains an elite policy meant for promoting corporate interests, there can be little progress in policy implementation. Therefore, he argues it is essential that India and its South-Asian neighbours repose faith in their people and involve them in the process of economic integration of the nations.

Posing a pertinent question on the importance of Myanmar in India's Act East Policy, Munmun Majumdar is her article *Why Engaging Myanmar is important?*, argues that it would do well for India' Act East to convert North-East India's history and culture into a soft power resource. Therefore, the critical test for the success of India's Act East policy is to establish linkages between North-East India and Southeast Asia and therein lies to a great extent on New Delhi's ability to strengthen its ties with Myanmar. In the end it would be action at the level of implementation indeed that will determine the success or failure of this policy.

Sanjeeb Kakoti in his article *Engaging with ASEAN: Need for a Novel Approach* dwells upon the fact that artificial borders have created huge social, economic and ecological problems that have remained largely unattended. A combination of Systems Approach and Design Thinking could open up possibilities for reframing and invigorating the existing space IN THE context of intercourse between the NER and ASEAN.

Examining the social, economic, cultural and political perspectives of development in the state of Mizoram, K.V. Reddy in his article *The Act East Policy: Implications and Developmental Strategies in Mizoram* identifies the problems and prospects in the context of several developmental strategies that were initiated by the government. The Act East Policy is one such developmental strategy that incorporates the development of North-East Indian state of Mizoram. While the policy has completed two and half decades, the article argues that its local implications are hardly satisfactory.

P.P. Shrivastava in his article *Role of Culture in the Activation of the Act-East Policy* discusses the ways of building new symbiotic psychological and material super-structure of mutual friendliness, peace, prosperity, progress and happiness at people-to-people levels to give expression to the Act East Policy of India.

Arguing that the rebranding of India's Look East into Act East stems from regional developments such as the United States and China competing for regional supremacy, Konthoujam Sarda in her article *Closing the Chasm: India's transition from Looking East to Acting East* points out that in the domestic front the Act East policy is also pronounced in incorporating the North-East of India to be the gateway to South-East Asia through connectivity and infrastructural developments.

To sum up the essence of this volume, Ambassador Rajiv Bhatia (Retd.) in his Guest of Honour Speech at the ASEAN Studies Centre (ASC), Shillong inauguration very aptly elucidated it is important to be seen that India's Act East Policy is not new, but rather a policy up-gradation with the changing spirit of time, from the previously known "Look East Policy" and urged the government and the people to "look North-East to Act East", and it could not have been a more pertinent time to *Act East through the North-East*.

We are thankful to Smt. Preeti Saran, Secretary (East) and Smt. Pooja Kapur, Joint Secretary (ASEAN-ML) Ministry of External Affairs, Government of India for their earnest desire in setting-up the ASEAN Studies Centre at the ICSSR North Eastern Regional Centre, Shillong. We are also grateful to Professor S.K. Srivastava, Vice-Chancellor, NEHU and Chairman, ASC, Shillong who has been a great source of strength in organising this important event. We appreciate much for the contribution of all the panelists, particularly Ambassador Rajiv Bhatia. We thankfully acknowledge the help received from Professor L.S. Gassah, Honorary Director, ICSSR-NERC, the staff of NEHU, ICSSR-NERC and ASC for the success of the entire event. Mr. Rajan of Pentagoan Press deserves special thanks for bringing out this book in a very short notice.

C. JOSHUA THOMAS
KONTHOUJAM SARDA

1

Look East to Act East:
India's Economic Engagements with ASEAN

Prabir De

1. Introduction

India's strong civilisational and cultural links with the Southeast Asian countries date back thousands of years. India's engagement with the eastern neighbourhood in contemporary period has its origin in early 1990s when the country undertook the Look East Policy (LEP) as an effort to strengthen economic and strategic relations with Southeast and East Asian countries. While India's footprints in Southeast and East Asia have increased considerably over the past two decades, the overall performance has been somewhat mixed. Trade between India and Southeast and East Asia has declined in recent years amid a strong presence of physical and non-physical barriers. Investment flow has not picked up at the required pace. The weak connectivity of North Eastern Region (NER) of India with the rest of India and neighbouring countries has remained a serious deterrent to India's engagement with the East. Re-engaging with the Southeast and East Asia has, therefore, become necessary.

Unveiled in 2014, the Act East Policy (AEP) incorporates a greater degree of action and dynamism.[1] Under AEP, India aims to play a proactive role in Southeast and East Asia. Both ASEAN and India are keen to build a common market with an ambitious but realistic economic integration programme. The difference between LEP and AEP in terms of approach is that ASEAN is at the core of AEP. India's connectivity with ASEAN may turn out to be a great facilitator of pan-Asian integration in the coming years (Kimura and Umezaki, 2011; De, 2014).

Northeast India is centre of India's LEP/AEP. Northeast India has a rich heritage and natural resources. NER was industrialised as early as 1850s: tea gardens in Assam in 1835, Dibrugarh-Chittagong rail in 1880s, oil refinery in Digboy in 1901, and many more. Services driven, NER has eight resource rich states with abundant industrial space and vibrant neighbourhood. But, NER suffers from high transportation costs, away from main Indian market. Apparently, economic isolation plus high transportation costs slow down NER's growth. The AEP provides opportunities to NER to benefit from its vast border and vibrant neighbours (De and Majumdar, 2014; Das and Thomas, 2016).

It is often claimed that the regional integration process in Southeast Asia has been driven by market forces, with little support from formal institutional arrangements. However, the situation began to change when the ASEAN Free Trade Area (AFTA) was launched in 1993. The integration has gained momentum with implementation of various FTAs with the dialogue partners including the ASEAN-India FTA, which came into effect in 2010. Furthermore, ASEAN has taken a further step forward, transforming itself from a mere free-trade area into the ASEAN Economic Community (AEC), which could enhance the free movement of goods, services, investment, capital and skilled labour, and could contribute to the formation of single market as well as a single production base. ASEAN has embraced the AEC on 1st January 2016, albeit on a smaller scale. Simultaneously,

ASEAN has undertaken series of initiatives to achieve the AEC 2025 milestones. AEC comprises four pillars: a single market and production base, a highly competitive economic region, a region of equitable economic development, and a region fully integrated into the global economy, each has strong implications for India and other dialogue partners of ASEAN (Mikic, 2016).

This paper presents the emerging economic relations scenario between ASEAN and India. Further, the paper is organised as follows: *Section 2* presents current state of engagements between ASEAN and India. *Section 3* discusses ASEAN and India and the challenges. Conclusions are drawn in *Section 4*.

2. Current Engagements between ASEAN and India

India and ASEAN are home to 1.8 billion people and have an economic size of US$ 3.8 trillion and a substantial share of world resources, economic and otherwise.[2] Both share land and maritime boundaries with each other. India has signed several bilateral and regional trade agreements with Southeast Asia, in the form of FTAs, comprehensive economic cooperation agreements and comprehensive economic partnership agreements; of these, the FTA with ASEAN has been the most important in strengthening economic relations with Southeast Asia.[3] With a free-trade agreement (FTA) in goods in 2010, ASEAN and India have created a large economic area, the first major step towards creating an ASEAN-India regional trade and investment region. In 2016, both India and ASEAN completed their tariff liberalisation obligations. Although negotiations for a trade in services and investment agreement have been completed, it has yet to be implemented. At the same time, India is a partner of the Regional Comprehensive Economic Partnership (RCEP), which is a comprehensive free trade agreement being negotiated between the 10 ASEAN members and ASEAN's FTA partners, i.e., Australia, China, India, Japan, the Republic of Korea and New Zealand.[4]

The India-ASEAN relationship has entered its third decade.

India became a sectoral partner of ASEAN in 1992, a dialogue partner in 1996 and a summit-level partner at Phnom Penh in 2002. The ASEAN-India strategic partnership—the elevated relationship that began at the 2012 Commemorative Summit—gives greater hope for delivering stronger bilateral relations. The relationship between ASEAN and India was elevated to Strategic Partnership level in 2012. As a Strategic Partner of ASEAN, India is also actively associated with various ASEAN-led forums dealing with defence and strategic issues. These include the East Asia Summit, the ASEAN Regional Forum, the ASEAN Defence Ministers Meeting Plus and the Expanded ASEAN Maritime Forum. India's engagement with ASEAN has expanded rapidly. Today, India has 30 annual dialogue mechanisms with ASEAN, including a Summit and seven Ministerial level meetings in key sectors. ASEAN and India are celebrating their 25th year of dialogue partnership, 15 years of summit level partnership and 5 years of strategic partnership in 2017. (Table 1)

Out of US$ 65 billion in 2015-16 bilateral trade, India's export to and import from ASEAN were US$ 25.2 billion and US$ 39.8 billion, respectively. Despite geographical proximity and cultural affinity, trade and investment between ASEAN and India are substantially lower than the potential. The Free Trade Agreement (FTA) in goods, implemented in 2010, and the services trade and investment agreement in 2015 between ASEAN and India represent an important effort to enhance regional integration. India is also member of RCEP Agreement, which is presently being negotiated among ASEAN+6 countries. Till 2016, total 15 rounds of negotiations were held for RCEP Agreement.

At the sectoral level, ASEAN is India's fourth largest trade partner, next to EU, USA and China. ASEAN-India FTA has become a comprehensive trade agreement with the implementation of ASEAN-India services and investment agreement in 2015. As argued before, rising trade deficit and low utilisation of ASEAN-India FTA have been the major concerns. It

Table 1: Present Scenario of ASEAN-India Engagements

ASEAN-India FTA	• Completed with the entering into force of the Services and Investment agreement in 2015 •	• Bilateral trade: US$ 65 billion in 2015-16 (India's export to ASEAN US$ 25.2 billion, India's import from ASEAN US$ 39.8 billion) • Emerging value chain, but slowly • Rising trade deficit is a matter of concern Low utilisation of FTA
RCEP	• Being negotiated	• Till December 2016, total 15 rounds of RCEP negotiation were held.
Trade facilitation (e.g. Customs cooperation)	• Unilateral initiatives • WTO TFA	• ASEAN single window under implementation and India's SWIFT working already
ASEAN-India maritime transport agreement	• Being negotiated	• Target date of signing of agreement - 2017
ASEAN-India airtransport agreement	• Proposed	• High imbalance between carriers; major ASEAN airlines (e.g. SQ or TG) utilise 100% slots
Land transport	• Trilateral highway & extension to CLV • MIEC • Kaladan MMTTP	• Ongoing but slow pace • Must build strong backward linkages in India's NER
Digital network	• Optical fibre network between India and ASEAN	• Ongoing but slow pace

Source: Author's own.

is hoped that services trade agreement may facilitate India's exports to ASEAN, thereby narrowing the trade deficits.

Another important aspect of ASEAN-India trade is regional value chains. India is yet to witness the value chains with ASEAN in large way. The value chains are emerging, but slowly. For example, mobile phone, automobiles, computers, etc., are being manufactured in India with parts and components sourced from ASEAN countries, China and Taiwan.[5]

Trade facilitation, particularly in customs cooperation is an area where member countries of ASEAN and India have taken unilateral initiatives and are committed to initiate trade facilitation measures through the WTO Trade Facilitation Agreement (TFA). Most of the ASEAN countries including India are signatories of WTO TFA and have ratified the TFA. ASEAN Single Window is under implementation, whereas India's SWIFT has started working since 1 April 2016.[6] Both platforms should support the exchange of certificates of origin and advance cargo information. Nevertheless, inter-operability between the two single windows in customs will make trade faster and paperless.

ASEAN and India also share maritime border. Barring shipping links between India and Singapore or that between India and Malaysia, maritime connectivity between ASEAN and India is not yet fully developed.[7] ASEAN-India maritime transport agreement, which is presently being negotiated, is likely to be signed in 2017. ASEAN-India air transport agreement has been proposed. There has been high imbalance between carriers in ASEAN and India serving each other's regions. While major ASEAN airlines (e.g. SQ or TG) have already utilised the slots, airlines from India, particularly Air India, are yet to make any substantial entry into ASEAN. The 'Make-in-India' syndrome has been moving fast, and therefore connectivity over the Bay of Bengal is important. Since air cargo is growing faster than sea cargo, ASEAN and India need more airports.

Overland physical and digital networks between ASEAN and

India are the pillars of ASEAN-India integration.[8] In case of land transportation, work on Trilateral Highway (TH) has been going on with replacement of 69 old bridges between Tamu and Kalewa and construction of road between Kalewa and Yargi in Myanmar. Trilateral Highway is likely to be completed by 2020. India has also proposed extension of Trilateral Highway to Lao PDR, Vietnam and Cambodia. Besides, port and inland water transportation components of the Kaladan multimodal transit transport project are almost ready. Myanmar Port Authority (MPA) is likely to take over the redeveloped Sittwe port. The connecting road inside Myanmar and India as part of Kaladan project are also getting ready. The Detailed Project Report (DPR) for construction of road between Rih and Tidim (82 km) has been completed.

The Trilateral Motor Vehicle Agreement (MVA) is being negotiated. This Agreement will allow vehicles and passengers to move seamlessly for regional and international trade transportation purposes along the Trilateral Highway. The MVA will provide a series of procedures that will facilitate movement of cargo and passengers along the corridors, such as operating procedures for vehicles, customs procedures, etc., and facilitation measures. The MVA will also provide the transit and transportation rights and obligations through Annexes and Protocols. This agreement will play a critical role in realising the seamless movement of passenger, personal and cargo vehicles along the Trilateral Highway.

India is planning to set up the Sittwe Economic Zone (SEZ). This economic zone is proposed to be located at Ponnar Kyun, 18 km upstream of Sittwe port in Myanmar. Myanmar government has identified about 1833 acres of land at Ponnar Kyun for the economic zone. Agro and fisheries are likely to have a good development potential in the region. This economic zone may accommodate industrial projects, which will cater to the local and larger Indian and Southeast Asian markets.

Mekong–India Economic Corridor (MIEC) is another important

connectivity project that aims to connect South Asia (India) with Southeast Asia (Vietnam) cutting across Thailand and Cambodia. Mainly a Japanese initiative, this corridor aims to strengthen the connectivity between South and Southeast Asia.[9] The emphasis of the corridor is on expanding the manufacturing base and trade with the rest of the world, particularly with India. The corridor will enable economies of ASEAN and India to integrate further and collectively emerge as a globally competitive economic bloc.

India is also setting up fibre optic network between India and ASEAN countries. While the physical work of laying the network is not yet started, the tele-medicine or tele-education part of the project has been ongoing and has received high welcome in ASEAN.

ASEAN and India are not doing much on the energy sector cooperation. India and ASEAN have to connect their energy grids. In view of our SDG commitments, more sustainable energy projects, particularly solar energy, are good for both the regions. Several ASEAN countries are part of International Solar Alliance project. We may consider reviving the India-Myanmar-Bangladesh gas pipeline project.

In addition, the MIEC and the Sittwe Economic Zone are two important projects that would facilitate multimodal connectivity and investment. India's Prime Minister has announced a special facility of US$ 1 billion to promote projects that support physical and digital connectivity between India and ASEAN, with particular focus on Mekong countries.

What follows India's regional connectivity with Southeast Asia has been evolving on two pillars—northeast India for multimodal and intermodal operations and southern India for multimodal operation. At present, several connectivity projects have been ongoing. Once connectivity projects start attracting investment, engages into the development of the region and improves the quality of life of the local people through generation of employment and reduction of poverty, these projects then become a truly public good and then turn to be economic corridors.

3. ASEAN-India Trade: Ways to Bring the Momentum

World is in the throes of uncertainty. A gloomy outlook is enveloping the world's economies. Weak global demand has started reducing Asia's exports. Global trade growth remains below 3 percent in 2015.[10] Exports of Asian open economies having strong links in global value chains have been slowing faster. Slowing Chinese economy is rippling across Asia, and there is rising tide of protectionism across the world. At the same time, bilateral trade between ASEAN and India has declined to US$ 66 billion in 2015, compared to US$ 75 in 2014. Figure 1 captures a sharp decline in India's export to and import from ASEAN since 2014. India's export to major markets has decelerated between 2000 and 2014, and in some particular markets like China India's export has even witnessed negative growth (Figure 2). The biggest challenge is to check the fall in trade and bring it back to normal level. There are three primary reasons for such a decline.

Figure 1: Trends in India's Trade with ASEAN (US$ Billion)

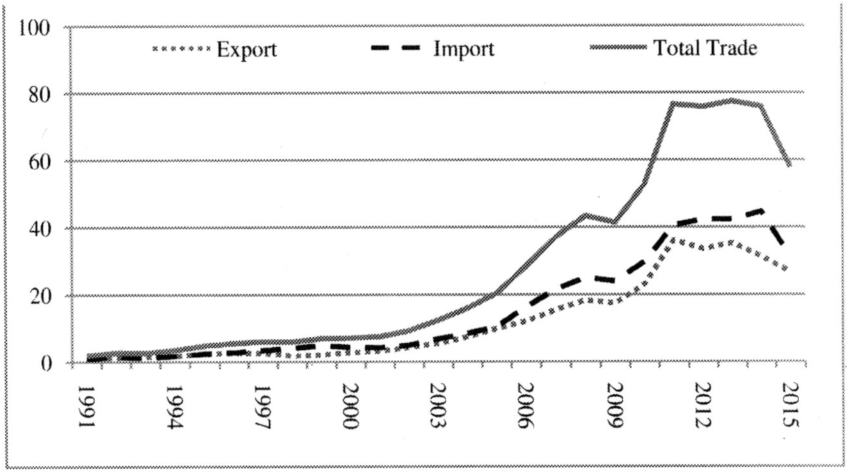

Source: Author based on DOTS, IMF.

Figure 2: India's Trade with Major Economies (US$ billion)

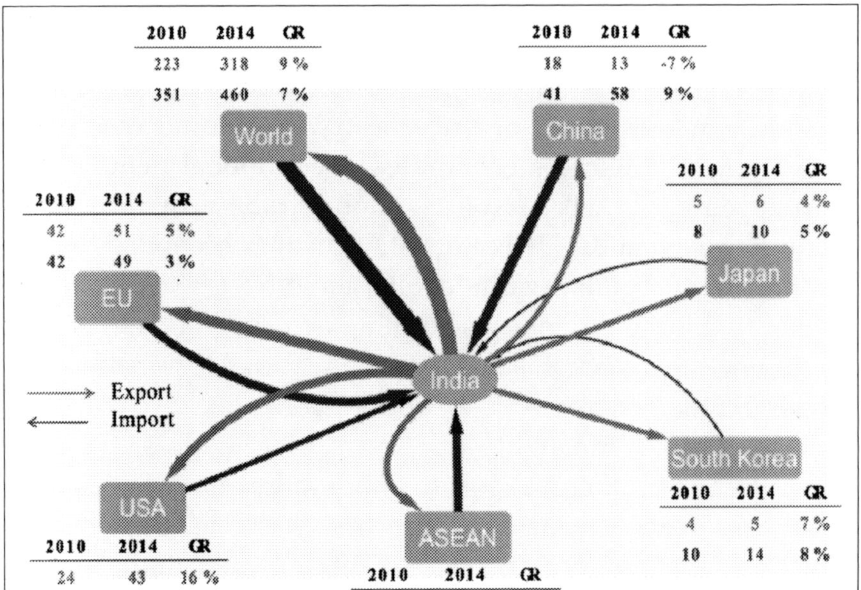

Source: AIC based on DOTS, IMF

First, fall in commodity prices in major petroleum products such as diesel have affected the dollar earnings from exports of refined petroleum products like diesel and petrol trade, resulting in falling Indian exports to ASEAN.

Second, as illustrated in Figure 3, ASEAN's market size has been shrinking in recent years duc to structural changes in China's import demand. As a spiralling effect, ASEAN is importing less from India.

Third, China's shift of import demand from labour/resource intensive to capital intensive goods has made India perplexed. India is yet to transform to meet the new import demand in ASEAN and China.

Figure 3: ASEAN's Trade with Major Economies (US$ billion)

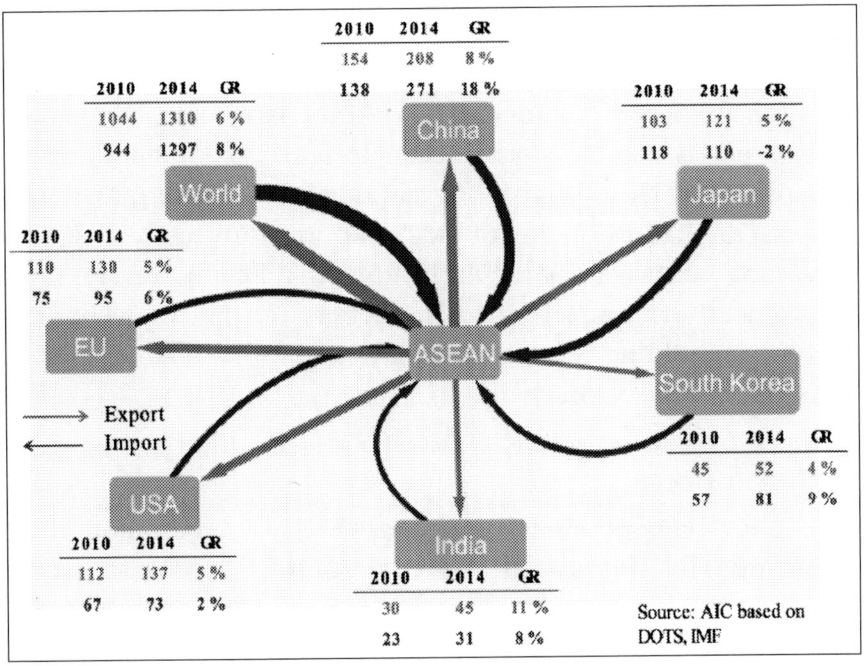

Given India's narrow base of merchandise exports, its export basket is no longer as price elastic as it once was because of close substitutes of products supplied by other countries. At the same time, India's merchandise exports are facing declining price competitiveness due to inadequate transport infrastructure and trade facilitation measures. Indian exporters to ASEAN are unable to improve the export margin due to high trade costs due to poor infrastructure, non-tariff measures (NTMs), etc. Exports incentives are too negligible to compensate for the additional cost incurred on account of poor trade infrastructure. On top, India's major exports have been facing prohibitive NTMs in ASEAN. In some ASEAN countries, where tariffs are lower, India's exports are subject to heavy NTMs. Therefore, it could be easily guessed why the utilisation of ASEAN-India FTA has been low. Therefore, to enhance the trade between India and ASEAN, both the countries need to remove the impediments to trade and investment, such as the high non-tariff barriers, lack of connectivity (physical, digital and social) and regulatory barriers. India and ASEAN have to strengthen regional connectivity and integration, particularly through cross-border infrastructure. At the same time, India needs to expand its manufacturing sector to boost exports and ensure sustainability. The decline in the manufacturing sector growth rate has cast its shadow on the country's exports, causing them to slow down in recent years, particularly after 2011. Finally, development of connectivity must lead to the generation of new economic activities. Building connectivity may help India to strengthen its manufacturing sector.

4. Conclusions

This paper suggests that India and ASEAN are becoming more economically integrated and that there is ample scope for deepening this integration process. Given India's diversity and geographical contrasts, an integrated transport network with Southeast Asia in particular is required to support the integration process. Asia-wide connectivity projects such as the Asian Highway and Trans-Asian Railway will be complemented by cross-border transport projects linking India with Southeast Asia, such as the Trilateral Highway. In addition, harmonisation of the policy, legal and regulatory regimes between India and ASEAN is needed. Stronger connectivity across NER will build a stronger network of cross-border production chains, particularly with Southeast Asia and Bangladesh. The development of economic corridors taking countries in the region will facilitate investments as well as spur economic growth in India's southern and northeastern regions as well as in Myanmar and the Mekong countries.

Automobile, pharmaceutical, machinery, electronics are the sectors which can be promoted to develop relational model with the lead firms, thereby strengthening the production networks between ASEAN and India. To facilitate the production networks, free flow of investment and movement of skilled labourers across the region are must.

Implementation matters mere signing of the FTA is not enough. In implementing FTAs, we need to keep in mind that regional integration can only be successful if it unleashes new competition that lowers prices, introduces new technology and gains productivity. Both ASEAN and India have been facing several challenges, which are quite obvious. It is also quite usual that FTA may give rise to negative effects, including rise in poverty and inequality, when variations exist in economic and social sectors. These effects should be identified and appropriate measures should be taken to address them. Coordinated efforts are necessary to realise sustainable growth and development in India and Southeast Asia. Good coordination among countries, national line ministries, regional sector institutions and other stakeholders is essential. Besides, harmonising political, legal and regulatory regimes between India and ASEAN is needed.

Under the Act East Policy, investment potential may considerably go up in NER, when we consider its geographical proximity to Southeast and East Asian markets. Time is ripe for India to establish a strong economic partnership with ASEAN. While this will reinforce India's security, it would also gradually remove economic isolation of India's NER.

ENDNOTES

1. Speech of by the Indian Prime Minister at the twelfth AEAN-India Summit, held at Nay Pyi Thaw, Myanmar on 12 November 2014, Available at www.mea.gov.in/Speeches-Statements.htm?dtl/24236/ Remarks_by_ the_ Prime_Minister_at_12th_IndiaASEAN_Summit_Nay_Pyi_Taw_Myanmar).
2. Based on the World Bank's World Development Indicators (WDI).
3. India's FTA with ASEAN was signed on 13 August 2009 and came in effect in January 2010.
4. Some of the key subjects that have been discussed in the working groups are tariff modalities in goods, listing of services and investment, elements of the RCEP chapters and possible texts, intellectual property, competition, economic

and technical cooperation, legal and institutional issues, customs procedures and trade facilitation, and rules of origin. The latest RCEP trade negotiation was held in New Zealand in 2016.

5. Refer, for example, Nag (2016).
6. The ASEAN Single Window currently supports the exchange of the intra-ASEAN certificate of origin (ATIGA Form D) and ASEAN Customs Declaration Document (ACDD) on a pilot basis among seven Member States and will be expanded to exchange other types of data.
7. Refer, AIC (2014).
8. Refer, for example, François et al. (2009), Kimura and Umezaki (2011), RIS (2012), De (2014), etc., which have dealt extensively various facets of ASEAN-India connectivity.
9. Refer, for example, Bhattacharyay et al. (2012)
10. Refer, World Trade Statistical Review 2016, WTO

REFERENCES

ADB and ADBI (2009). *Infrastructure for Seamless Asia*, Asian Development Bank, Manila, and Asian Development Bank Institute, Tokyo.

AIC – RIS (2015) *ASEAN-India Development and Cooperation Report 2015*, ASEAN-India Centre (AIC) - Research and Information System for Developing Countries (RIS), New Delhi: Routledge, AIC (2014) *ASEAN – India Maritime Connectivity Report*, ASEAN – India Centre (AIC), New Delhi

Bhattacharyay B., R. Nag and M. Kawai (2012). *Infrastructure for Asian Connectivity.* ADBI, Tokyo, and Edward Elgar, Cheltenham, United Kingdom.

De, P (2014) 'India's Emerging Connectivity with Southeast Asia: Progress and Prospects', Working Paper 507, Asian Development Bank Institute (ADBI), Tokyo

De, P. and M. Majumdar (2014). *Developing Cross-Border Production Networks between India's North Eastern Region of India, Bangladesh and Myanmar: A Preliminary Assessment.* Research and Information System for Developing Countries, New Delhi.

De, Prabir and Suthiphand Chirathivat (2016) *Celebrating the Third Decade and Beyond: New Challenges to ASEAN-India Economic Partnership*, New Delhi: Knowledge World.

Francois, J.F., G. Wignaraja and P. Rana (2009). *Pan-Asian Integration: Linking East and South Asia*, New York: Palgrave Macmillan..

Kimura, F. and S. Umezaki (2011) *ASEAN–India Connectivity: The Comprehensive Asia Development Plan (CAPD) Phase 2*, Economic Research Institute of ASEAN and East Asia (ERIA), Jakarta

Mikic, Mia (2016) "Trade Implications of the ASEAN+ Agreements for Other Asian Countries", in Mia Mikic and Bruno Jetin (eds.) *ASEAN Economic Community: A Model for Asia-wide Regional Integration?* New York: Palgrave Macmillan.

Nag, Biswajit (2016) "India-ASEAN Production Networks: What is There for Indian SMEs?", in De and Chirathivat (2016)

Plummer, Michael, Peter J. Morgan, and Ganeshan Wignaraja (2015) *Connecting Asia: Infrastructure for Integrating South and Southeast Asia*, Edward Elgar, Cheltenham

RIS (2012) *ASEAN – India Connectivity Report: India Country Study*, Research and Information System for Developing Countries (RIS), New Delhi

2

Maritime Perspectives of India's Act East Policy and its Implications for India's Emerging Consensus of Engagement

W. Lawrence S. Prabhakar

India's 'Act East' Policy and engagement has been the pivotal engagement of India's Southeast Asia, East Asia and Asia-Pacific engagement. Given the continental and maritime geopolitics vistas of this engagement its importance and impact on the scope and salience of this initiative has substantial implications for India's trade, transport, people movement and in the overall frameworks of connectivity, regional and sub-regional cooperation initiatives like BIMSTEC, BCIM. Its leveraging impetus is now evident in the burgeoning trade and investment that has been on the two-way process between India and ASEAN.

The holistic scope of India's Act East lies in the development of trade and transport connectivity linked with sustainable regional development accounts for the continental and maritime dimensions of its engagement with ASEAN and beyond. The

India-ASEAN economic engagement and security convergence shaped India's perception of the Asia-Pacific security architecture that is now increasingly aligned with the larger canvas of Asian geopolitics deriving from the continental geopolitics, which is the India-China theatre and the maritime geopolitics of the Indian and Pacific Oceans. (Tellis and Mirsk, 2013). India's responses and options have been through the diplomatic processes of engaging with ASEAN with ARF and ADMM Plus.

Economic, commercial, trade interdependence and security cooperation have been the intertwining sources of India's ASEAN engagement. In its continental terrain, India's Northeast constitutes the pivot of its regional development, regional cooperation and trans-border trade and investments with Myanmar and Thailand; while Peninsular India has been engaged in its ancient maritime civilisational and trade linkages with archipelagic Southeast Asia.

The new impetus in India's Act East Policy in its contemporary contexts needs a salient historical-cultural-civilizational connect like the Tamil Chola connect; much like how China exploits the Ming Dynasty's legendary Admiral Zheng He's long voyages to South India and East Africa, which is today repositioned as the Belt-Road Initiative (BRI). This rejuvenated emphasis on the historic–civilisational, cultural vistas would infuse the diaspora and trade constructs and would thus galvanize the engaging dynamism of trade, investment; auguring efforts in regional development and cooperation. Project Mausam is one such initiative proposed, yet has to take shape that would envisage a vista for the Indian Ocean regional cultural-trade system; India thus needs yet another historic–civilisational paradigm that would rediscover the comprehensive connectivity with Southeast Asia both from its continental Northeast land connectivity and the peninsular India's maritime connectivity that would 'celebrate' its cultural renaissance and leverage for greater interdependence.

In elucidating the maritime contexts of India's Act East Policy in its historical quintessence, it is essential to examine the detailed salience of Ancient Tamil Culture and civilization in Southeast Asia from the perspective of the Tamil Empire of the Cholas who embarked on a grand vision of Southeast Asia of conquest, trading posts and colonial outposts intertwined with culture and civilisational footprint in the region. It saw the emergence of a Pan-Tamil empire of Sri Lanka and Southeast Asia in the waterways of South China Sea was chequered with Chola naval warships and merchant marine (Kulke, Kesavapany, Sakhuja, 2009). The continued Indian presence in the region has been due to the naval expeditions, trading and settlements in the region that resulted in the enduring historical social and cultural ties. In its contemporary essence, the imperative for India is to envision a holistic civilisational and cultural paradigm that has salient "soft power" accents into the region and on to the East Pacific—in the quest for "Act East". India's "Look East" and "Act East". Such a paradigm could emerge from the rich history of the Tamil Civilisational connect of the Cholas with Southeast Asia.

In the contemporary post-colonial period, India's first diplomatic initiative was the Asian Relations Conference in 1947 in New Delhi and followed by the Bandung Conference in 1955. The Asian Relations Conference and the Bandung Conference were the initial foundation stones of the emerging Asian security order that was envisaged and built by India and Indonesia (See Seng, Tan & Acharya, 2008). But the Indian quest to sustain this engagement was diverted due to its threats from Pakistan and China through the years 1947-1991 and continued on. In the post-Cold War period, India's return to Southeast Asia with its "Look East Policy" in the early 1990s, saw a rechristened India—chastened by the twists of the Cold War dynamics returns as a regional power with colossal economic potential and an emerging security bulwark. This transition also featured the realities of the new power balance in the region between India and Southeast Asia leaving behind the hubris of its past engagement with its Southeast Asia in the past (Ayoob, 1990).

Yet in a different context, the ASEAN and its economic policies had also resulted in the new benchmarks for India's own pathways on economic reforms. This 'turning of tables for India' with Southeast Asia and ASEAN was also reflected in the fact that not all members of ASEAN were enthusiastic about bringing New Delhi into the regional institutions due to the largely hectoring moral planks of India's Foreign Policy and diplomacy that had been its staple engagement (Brewster, 2012:157–60).

To elucidate the contexts of India's Act East in Southeast Asia, it is essential to locate the axis of India's geopolitics in the region.

The Continental and Maritime Quintessence of India's Act East

India's unique geo-spatial profile of its continental borders/ boundaries and maritime boundaries projects to Southeast Asia from its land-borders to maritime boundaries. India's Northeast is thus the land geo-pivot of its engagement with Myanmar. Thailand with its ancient historical and cultural ties—an indispensable historical reality that has been long overlooked for years (Sailo, 2012). The Northeast of India and its natural geographical land corridor connectivity with Southeast Asia has been the pivot of spontaneous interchange of migration, settlement, transmission of culture and civilisation.

The continental geopolitics of the region projects the Northeast as the critical junction in the borders with China and Southeast Asia. With Southeast Asia it has common land borders with Burma and Thailand. The geographical 'China connect' in this region has been a tremendous source of the shaping and influencing of the region's identity as well as sustained trade and commerce since ancient times and the transmission of culture and identity. Thus 'social constructions' of ethnic and lingual identities have a larger imprint of China and Southeast Asia in the region. As the colonial and post-colonial state making and map making construction projects began, the natural civilisational identities of ethnicity and nation were forcibly subsumed to a larger identity that has not been holistically reflective of the regional cultures and identities (Zou and Kumar, 2011). Land corridors have an enduring permanence of culture and identity transmission and its maintenance given the permanence of identities across the borders. India's Northeast's natural engagement with Southeast Asia and China are thus spontaneous with the regional identities and their histories that have been largely ignored by the mainstream dominant discourses (Senz and Reinhardt, 2014). In the present contexts, the regional and sub-regional identities and histories of the regions are artificially demarcated by borders and boundaries that are reflective of post-colonial India rather than the cultural civilisational continuum of the historical past.

India's Coromandal South—Peninsular India engagement in the maritime corridor of Bay of Bengal to South China Sea is the second axis of engagement with Southeast Asia. India's Southeast Asia axis has long and enduring historical ties with the region that saw the imprints of ancient colonialization, trade, settlements and to the modern colonial period of Indian and Tamil labour settling in the various countries of Malaysia, Singapore and Indonesia (Ting, 2009) The maritime geopolitics of this engagement saw the role of Tamils and other nationalities playing a vital role in the nation-building of the countries of Southeast Asia besides their role in the defence of the region during World War II. In the post-1990s, with the Look East Policy, India's engagement increased with several trans-regional economic and trade partnerships. Maritime trade, maritime security and the imperatives to secure sea lanes of communication both energy-laden and cargo-laden shipping from a host of maritime asymmetric threats and challenges emerged as important priorities for India and Southeast Asia (Brewster, 2014). India's maritime connect with Southeast Asia was through the Andaman and Nicobar islands archipelago chain, which provides an important hub of people movement through into Thailand and Malaysia.

Thus in its contemporary contexts, India's Northeast and Peninsular South especially the Coromandel seaboard along with Andaman and Nicobar Islands predominantly offer the economic-commercial-trade people movement and security convergence with Southeast Asia. The emerging trade, transport corridors, infrastructure investment connectivity spawn the entire gamut of India's Act East engagement that is now catalyzing the transformation of the region (Palit, 2008; 2015a) The Continental and Maritime corridors axes with Southeast Asia has resulted in expansion of India's engagement with the Asia-Pacific (continental) and the Indo-Pacific (maritime) with its new and existing regional and transregional networks of organisations. While roads and railroads now link Northeast with Southeast Asia for energy and trade flows, India's robust Navy and its burgeoning merchant marine engages South China Sea in trade and transit thus providing the security dividend of the region (Prabhakar, 2013).

India and ASEAN Comprehensive Political and Security Engagement

The convergence between India and ASEAN in its political and security dimensions emerged from the transforming Asia-Pacific security canvas that has witnessed China's rise, the imperatives of ASEAN to balance China with India and the importance to enmesh India and China in their economic potential with ASEAN. The importance of enmeshment of India was the catalyst for ASEAN to engage with India with the objectives of expanding connectivity and investments. The importance of the continental and maritime axes of geopolitics has been the catalyzing and enabling factor in the comprehensive political and security engagement between India and ASEAN.

India's 'Look East Policy' announced in 1992 was aimed to tap into the emerging robust Southeast Asian economies. This exercise was intertwined with the imperatives of India to strengthen economic and security cooperation with the region (Mun, 2009).

The region given its geographical contiguity of India's intermediate neighbourhood is evident with its land borders with Myanmar, Thailand and the maritime borders with Malaysia and Indonesia (Prabhakar, 2014a). India's Look East Policy energized the reception of India by ASEAN into several of its forums and encompassing areas of engagement in politics and security.

Geographical borders and contiguous areas had also necessitated India to forge closer ties with Southeast Asia in the domain of security cooperation. Perhaps the primary catalyst of the expanded India-ASEAN security convergence and cooperation has been China's growing influence in the region. Given the fact that India shares maritime boundaries with Indonesia, Myanmar and Thailand and perceives any disturbance or external intervention in this area as a potential threat, the India-Southeast Asia maritime exchanges and naval exercises have emerged as an important feature (Prabhakar, 2014b). On the other hand, border security has been one of the primary issues in the land borders that India has with Southeast Asia.

Since 1990s, India and ASEAN have been promoting "long-term cooperative partnership" in security cooperation in order to construct a stable and peaceful region. Given the region's increasing security turbulence and the increasing frequencies of uncertainties resulting from major power competition, territorial disputes, and non-traditional security threats, the imperative between ASEAN and India in areas of comprehensive security cooperation and dialogue has intensified.

India and ASEAN have reached a level of mutual understanding at varying levels of strategic interaction on the need to combat international terrorism, transnational crimes, and other non-traditional security threats. While the strategic understanding has been very good between the political establishments, there are still areas in the tactical and operational levels where India and ASEAN would have to work harder to widen the scope of their security cooperation in the area of intelligence exchange, communication procedure, and law enforcement coordination (Singh, Bilveer, 2011; 2015)

India's Act East is well exemplified in its maritime doctrines that focuses on the primary areas of strategic interest in the maritime domain; this is well elucidated in its Maritime Military Strategy (2007). India's maritime vision and reach to the Indian and Pacific Oceans are linked by the Strait of Malacca. India in its Act East maritime vision has been emphasising and used the ASEAN Regional Forum and ASEAN-India Vision Statement to articulate its security stake in the South China Sea and announce its support for the liberal norms of freedom of navigation, principles of international law, and cooperation in maritime security. Through deft Diplomacy and the collective ASEAN support the Indian endeavour had been energised. The Indian Navy has been operating regularly in the Eastern and Western Pacific. Frequent dispatches of naval task forces, deployments and port calls to friendly countries in the area have been growing (Sakhuja and Khuranna, 2015). The past decade, India has also strengthened its defence cooperation with the ASEAN and its individual members with many defence-related agreements and its participation in regional security forums like the ASEAN Regional Forum, the East Asian Summit and the ASEAN Defence Minister Meeting-PLUS.

India's maritime strategy published in 2004 is *Freedom to use the Seas* is in itself a soft power exercise (Singh, 2015). India has emphasized freedom of navigation on the sea including in the South China Sea. Anti-piracy, anti-poaching, counter infiltration and anti-trafficking underpin the Indian Navy's constabulary role (Singh, Abhijit, 2012). The maritime doctrine and the outlined tasks exemplify India's potential soft power bases even though they involve the use of force.

India with various compatible interests with ASEAN states like the freedom of navigation and tackling non-traditional issues like piracy and terrorism has forged several partnerships with

Southeast Asian states. India signed a Joint Declaration for Cooperation to Combat International Terrorism in October 2003. While reiterating to implement effectively the agreement on combating terrorism (Singh, 2008). India has committed to engage in greater security cooperation on traditional security issues, while agreeing to enhance maritime cooperation including through the ASEAN Maritime Forum on issues ranging from piracy to freedom of navigation (Scott, 2013).

India has an important shared cause and vision with ASEAN to maintain balance and stability. India's position serves to stabilise and does not disturb the open regional order. India's accession to the Treaty of Amity and Cooperation is qualified by its support to Southeast Asia Nuclear Weapon-Free Zone. India's engagement with the ARF has contributed to its image as a benign military power.

The India-ASEAN 2012 *Vision Statement* appreciates "India's role in ensuring regional peace and stability" for its accession to the TAC, and "active contribution" in the ASEAN+1, the ARF, the EAS and the ASEAN Defence Ministers' Meeting (ADMM) Plus.

Besides the ASEAN heads of states commended India in their 20th year of ASEAN-India celebration of dialogue partnership in 2012 issuing a *Vision Statement* expressing their satisfaction about ASEAN-India Dialogue Relations and declared that the "Partnership stands elevated to a strategic partnership". ASEAN has strongly considered India as security partner with the *Vision Statement* reiterating joint commitments to cooperate on terrorism and maritime security.

In its 'Act East' maritime policy focus, India looks beyond the ASEAN-led architecture to consolidate its sphere of influence in the Indian Ocean with the Indian Ocean Rim Association (IORA) and Indian Ocean Naval Symposium (IONS) a maritime security forum and cooperation. The IORA is a multi-nation broad-spectrum cooperation initiative similar to BIMSTEC and includes countries around the Indian Ocean across continents. The IORA

(1997) and the IONS (2008) were initiated by India to include major Southeast Asian countries, namely Indonesia, Malaysia, Singapore and Thailand.

India's initiatives of the *Milan* and the Indian Ocean Naval Symposium *IONS* have accrued the institutional value addition to the prevalent ties and have fostered better naval engagement providing India 'a naval corridor in the South China Sea all the way to the East Pacific' to engagements with Japan, South Korea, Russia and the United States.

India's maritime multilateralism with Southeast Asia has all the elements of the benign scope of building maritime security in the region. It elucidates the rights of India to trade and transit in the South China Sea and also builds the legs of its quest to the Northeast Pacific and Eastern Pacific (Prabhakar, 2014c). India's engagement in ASEAN Defence Ministers Meeting in the ADMM Plus is an institutional initiative that encompasses India's security stakes in the region. India's trade and commerce as well as its ambitions to build the Arctic presence and bolster the Indo-Pacific presence motivate the Eastward expansion and consolidation.

India's Defence Diplomacy with ASEAN

India's ASEAN Diplomacy is primarily based on Defence diplomacy or the peacetime cooperative use of armed forces and its related infrastructure deployed as a tool of foreign and security policy has been increasingly employed by India since the 1990s with respect to Southeast Asian countries augmenting cooperation. India's Defence Diplomacy has been largely in terms of capacity-building of the service personnel of the armed forces of the Southeast Asian countries—training and building operational readiness to the armed forces.

India's Defence diplomacy in Southeast Asia covers a broad range of activities that includes Ministry of Defence training courses and education programmes training opportunities for overseas military cadets and officers who attend courses at India's military training establishments; it features the loan service personnel, short-term training teams, and civilian and military advisers being deputed to foreign governments for extended periods. Besides, it features the routine deployment of naval task forces and its symbolism of benign exercises and various constabulary and humanitarian and disaster relief missions at sea.

The naval defence diplomacy involves the Naval warships visits on port calls; deployment of military aircraft and other military units; the itinerant inward and outward visits by ministers and by military and civilian personnel at all levels; the routine of the Staff talks, conferences and seminars to improve mutual understanding and exercises that enhance cooperation and interoperability are the various measures that enhance naval interoperability of the Indian Navy with the ASEAN Navies.

The Cold War in the mid-eighties witnessed the huge India's military buildup that caused much anxiety among Southeast Asian nations. Southeast Asia was also initially apprehensive of India's expanded regional role and viewed India's role in Sri Lanka, Maldives and in Nepal radiating threats to their neighbourhood. The naval expansion saw the concomitant buildup of India's defence infrastructure buildup of the major naval base in Andaman and Nicobar Islands in late 1980s as a means to position and project naval and air power into the region. This development perturbed Indonesia and other littoral neighbours about India's potential power projection capabilities closer to their territorial waters. However, in the post-Cold War period and with the greater regional integration between India and Southeast Asia, the strategic importance of India has increased attracted immense attention in regard to India's naval modernisation programme évident in the light of India's power projection capabilities into Southeast Asia.

The consistent stand of India with the various diplomatic initiatives did assuage the Southeast Asian states about India's benign interests towards Southeast Asia and it has resulted in the gradual reduction of Southeast Asian apprehensions towards India over the years. This has been well buttressed by the fact that India has been most willing to engage in naval exercises and other defence diplomacy cooperation initiatives with the Southeast Asian region. India has been holding joint naval exercises with ASEAN states, viz. Singapore, Indonesia and Malaysia. Several training programmes initiatives and liaison visits had resulted in the consolidation to further confidence building between India and Southeast Asia.

These have been built on the sinews of the earlier links since the 1950s. Defence cooperation in the maritime/naval domain has often been the exception to this state of affairs. India's land and maritime engagement with Southeast Asia commences with Burma given the contiguity of the two countries' maritime borders besides the proximity of India's Andaman and Nicobar archipelago to Thailand and the Malacca strait. Thailand has 894 km of Andaman coastline, which rests within India's area of strategic influence. Several benign and constabulary exercises have been evident.

The Royal Thai Navy and the Indian Navy have been conducting an annual Indo-Thai Joint Working Group (JWG) Meeting since 2003. In 2008 the two navies initiated a bilateral Navy Staff Talk to cooperate in maritime security. The two navies are also engaging in joint patrolling or Coordinated Patrol (CORPAT) in the Andaman Sea. India and Thailand have also been sharing maritime intelligence and domain awareness in coordination with Singapore, Malaysia and Indonesia on patrolling and other movements in the Strait of Malacca and the Andaman Sea. The biennial MILAN naval exercise being hosted by the Indian Navy (IN) since 1995 has been a very important maritime security and defence diplomacy initiative in the region.

India has been a major source of military training for the ASEAN states. All the ASEAN countries are partners under the Indian Technical and Economic Cooperation (ITEC) programme offering defence training among others. India's military assistance to some ASEAN states also involves defence supplies and maintenance support. India's defence agreements with Singapore, Vietnam, Indonesia, Malaysia, Thailand and Philippines have broadened the scope of future defence cooperation.

The *2009 Indian Maritime Doctrine*, enunciates that "Naval diplomacy entails the use of naval forces...to build 'bridges of friendship' and strengthen international cooperation on the one hand, and to signal capability and intent to deter potential adversaries on the other." India's naval diplomacy resulted in the initiation of the IONS in 2008 featuring Singapore, Indonesia, Malaysia, Thailand, Myanmar participating as members. It aims at developing "friendship, cooperation and mutual understanding" MILAN is another Indian initiative. India has become part of the Regional Cooperation Agreement on Combating Piracy and Armed Robbery against ships in Asia (ReCAAP) with the Indian Coast Guard representing India. The Western Pacific Naval Symposium provides yet another forum for India to engage the Southeast Asian navies for cooperative security. The various naval operational initiatives and doctrinal templates envisage for a greater India-Southeast Asian maritime convergence that fosters India's maritime-based economic and forward security engagement (Singh, 2009; 2010).

The Indian Navy's exercises with Southeast Asian navies have varied levels of scope with the different naval forces of the regions. The Indian Navy had tasked its naval operations in varying levels engaging different platforms and capabilities with the objective to develop capacity for interoperability with the various Southeast Asian navies. Southeast Asian navies are varied in force architecture and capabilities based on different operational capacities and platform capabilities. Interoperability may not be feasible with the vast differences in training, operations and platforms, yet the exercises with each of the navies provide the Indian navy familiarity of operations and development of capacity. Although the exercises cannot accrue real offensive capability, the scope in terms of cooperative and constabulary elements remains high. From the Indian Navy's point of view, these exercises enhance maritime domain awareness, sharing of maritime intelligence and the benign scope of ties.

India's role in the region is expanding in terms of how its presence and partnerships could shape the Asian security architecture that has important strategic implications. India's impératives lie in sustaining its economic development and growth that are sustainable and are competitive with strong proaction in economic, commercial and technological partnerships with Southeast Asia ARF and with Japan, South Korea and Australia. The scope and sustenance of enduring partnerships with these powers encompassing a crucial system-shaping diplomatic synergy of India is extremely vital for India to be seriously reckoned in the region. Having assessed the intense and rich salience of India's Defence Diplomacy with Southeast Asia, it is important to analyse India's stakes and commitment in the region particularly the prospects of future cooperation and convergence.

Prospects of Future Cooperation and Convergence

The primary focus of India-ASEAN ties have been overwhelmingly economic cooperation, trade and commerce and the mutual patterns of investing in each other's economies. This has resulted in the considerable buildup of institutional frameworks, protocols and processes. The India-ASEAN maritime convergence has created a momentum that has a functionalist impact on security cooperation well intertwined with economics. In terms of security cooperation, India's shared maritime borders with Indonesia and Thailand and the land borders through India's Northeast with Myanmar brings to focus the close and joint concerns of security interests and issues in the areas of counter-terrorism, anti-piracy, counter-narcotics, and sea-lane security and protection.

The Strait of Malacca has been the primary maritime jugular

for India and Southeast Asia connecting Indian Ocean with South China Sea that funnels into the East Pacific. India's trade and transit interests in the Pacific is now an increasing geo-economic and hence a geostrategic priority. India's Energy Security is also sourced from the Russian Sakhalin transiting the waters of the South China Sea. India and Southeast Asia face the two primary threats of the Chinese assertiveness in the South China Sea and also the various maritime asymmetric threats from the region. Indian naval presence in the region in the form of bilateral exercises and frequent deployments enhances the security of passage of Indian shipping

A second area of India-ASEAN cooperation is focused to tackle terrorism and organised crime security threats is yet another important agenda in the growing bilateral relations. This has been strengthened by the earlier protocol of the 2003 Joint Declaration on Cooperation to Combat International Terrorism. India-ASEAN convergence has emerged in the area of borders and conflict management in respect of various insurgent groups that are operating out of Myanmar in India's Northeast. India solicits cooperation with the Myanmar government and with ASEAN. Similarly, the narcotics smuggling into India's Northeast from Myanmar intertwined with insurgency and small and light weapons is posing a major menace to India and ASEAN. This area could be a vital area of joint cooperation and also the impetus to facilitate the development of India's Northeast as the gateway to Southeast Asia for economic cooperation, trade and commerce and connectivity (Singh, 2011)

India-ASEAN convergence is also on non-traditional security in the areas of climate change and environmental security—as the intensity of natural disasters like sea-level rise inundating low level areas, tropical storms, prospect of future tsunamis, heat waves, etc. India-ASEAN convergence in humanitarian and disaster relief operations involving the navies and air forces would be new templates drawing cues from the Asian Tsunami 2004 relief and rehabilitation operations for future contingencies.

But the most important security convergence would come in the areas of traditional security as India and ASEAN face a highly assertive China that is now assertive to reclaim the entire swath of the South China Sea area as well as economically surmount the region with its dominant influence. India's strategic engagement in the region with enhanced economic cooperation and trade and commerce will go a very long way in cementing the regional order.

It is in this context that the Indian naval engagement with Southeast Asia assumes paramount significance. The Indian Navy's exercises with Southeast Asian navies have enhanced its capacity to present in the region:

(a) India is an extra-regional power that has vital commercial and economic interests with the countries of the South China Sea and has trade and transit routes through the South China Sea to its economic and commercial interests in the Russian Far East Sakhalin and the Pacific Rim countries—South China Sea is therefore a maritime route of trade and transit.

(b) As an extra-regional power, India's transit routes through the South China Sea are guaranteed under the Freedom of Navigation and are secured by International Maritime Law. Therefore, India aims for the development of a common understanding and common format for the acceptance and implementation of a "Code of Conduct" by which the peace and stability of the region is ensured among the regional and extra-regional powers.

(c) India's maritime engagements in the region have always been non-offensive and have nurtured cooperative and peaceful engagements with all states of Southeast Asia and beyond. The imperative for *cooperative maritime securities* ties with the regional states and among extra-regional states in pacific understanding are very vital in building stability and deterrence in the region.

(d) India is apprehensive of China's new maritime and air

assertiveness in the region that could encompass and could convert the South China Sea into a 'Chinese lake' by its forceful affirmation of territorial claims. India has a strong interest in maintaining domain awareness in all areas of maritime interests (Shambaugh, 2013; Vuwing, 2012).

(e) India's engagement in the South China Sea could come by way of *building operational safety* of the maritime capacities and platforms of the regional states. This measure is an important operational and navigational safety key mechanism that facilitates smooth maritime trade and transit of all littoral and extra-regional states who operate in the region. Regional bilateral and multilateral maritime dialogues could show the way for *the building maritime confidence and maritime stability* in the region that is wrought by various disputes.

From the Indian Navy's point of view, these exercises enhance maritime domain awareness, sharing of maritime intelligence and enhance the benign scope of ties. India's hosting of the MILAN and IONS reciprocally brings in the Southeast Asian navies to Indian waters for similar exercises that serve to enhance interoperable features of the various operational capacities of the different navies with the Indian Navy (Prabhakar, 2016). Interoperability serves as the benchmark of the closer degree of naval cooperation and operational capacity. The Indian Navy's operational capacity and its doctrinal focus endeavour towards greater cooperative capacity between its force and the navies in the region.

In summation, the analysis on India's engagement in Southeast Asia has been premised on India's growing economic trade, commercial investments, economic and trade interdependence that has directed the strategic engagement with the region. India's role in the region is expanding in terms of how its presence and partnerships could shape the Asian security architecture that has important strategic implications.

India's impératives lie in sustaining its economic development and growth that are sustainable and are competitive with strong proaction in economic, commercial and technological partnerships with Southeast Asia ARF and it expands eastward to Japan, South Korea and Australia. The scope and sustenance of enduring partnerships with these powers encompassing a crucial system-shaping diplomatic synergy of India is extremely vital for India to be seriously reckoned in the region.

India's Act East brings to fore a very crucial maritime economic and security synergy that is a crucial balancing role in the emerging prospective US-China high intense rivalry throughout the littoral and the maritime space of the Asia-Pacific. The Asia-Pacific economic and security regional order has been in turbulence in the last decade and in now entering into a new era of increased security dilemmas and strategic uncertainty with the impact of various critical destabilisation forces on Southeast Asia. India's 'Act East' would serve as a critical stabilising force as it would assure Southeast Asia, engage with China and enhance India's maritime trade and connectivity in the region. Given the discontents of an assertive China and a new dispensation of American power that is now recasting its future role and scope of its forward engagement. It is in this context that India's role and stabilising impact comes in its sustained maritime based "Act East" that would build the sinews of strength of a regional order that is not entirely swayed to the ruthless hegemony of China nor suffer from the pangs of the US strategic dilemma and decision of staying engaged in the region. India's normative leadership backed by its pragmatic calculus of economic strength and strategic capacity would provide the necessary foundations of India's proaction in Southeast Asia, East Asia and the Indo-Pacific.

REFERENCES

Ayoob, Mohammad, *India and South-East Asia: Indian Perceptions and Policies*, London: Routledge, 1990.

Brewster, David, 'India's Security Partnership with Singapore', *The Pacific Review* 11, 22 (5) 2009.

_______ *India as an Asia-Pacific Power Routledge Security in Asia Pacific*, Routledge: UK, 2012.

_______ "India's Engagements in Southeast Asia: Singapore, Vietnam and Indonesia," in, *The Engagement of India: Strategies and Responses*, Ian Hall (ed.), Washington, D.C.: Georgetown University Press, 2014a, pp. 147-68.

Mun, Chak, *India's Strategic Interests in Southeast Asia and Singapore*, Singapore: ISAS & Macmillan, 2009.

_______ "Singapore-India Strategic Relations: Singapore's Perspective," in *The Merlion and the Ashoka Singapore–India Strategic Ties*, Anit Mukherjee (ed.), Singapore: World Scientific, 2015.

Palit, Amitendu, 2008. "India-Singapore Trade Relations," ISAS Working Paper No. 46, 16 June accessed on 2 November 2015 at www.isn.ethz.ch/Digital-Library/Publications/Detail/?id=57282

_______ 2015a. "India-Southeast Asia Relations: Enhancing Mutual Benefits," New Delhi: Brookings India Impact Series, Foreign Policy accessed 10 October 2015 at http://www.brookings.in/wp-content/uploads/2015/06/India-Southeast-Asia-Relations-Amitendu.pdf

Prabhaker, W. Lawrence S., "India's Extended Maritime Mandala: Naval Intent and Strategy in Southeast Asia," in *India-ASEAN Defence Relations*, Ajaya K. Das (ed.), RSIS Monograph No. 28, 2013, Singapore: S. Rajaratnam School of International Studies accessed on 12 October 2015 at http://www.rsis.edu.sg/wp-content/uploads/2014/07/Monograph2813.pdf

_______ 2014a. "India and the Indo-Pacific," *Science, Technology Security Forum* accessed on 10 October 2015 at http://stsfor.org/content/india-and-indo-pacific

_______ "The Emergent Vistas of the Indo-Pacific," in *Indo-Pacific Region: Political and Strategic Prospects*, Rajiv K. Bhatia and Vijay Sakhuja, (eds.), New Delhi: Indian Council of World Affairs and Vij Books, 2014a, pp.10–12.

_______ 2014c 'India's Evolving Security Relations and Partnerships in the Indo-Pacific' in *Sea Change: Maritime Geopolitics in the Indo-Pacific Region*, David Michel & Ricky Paserelli (eds), Washington DC: The Henry Stimson Center, 2014. December accessed at https://www.files.ethz.ch/isn/189951/SEA-CHANGE-WEB.pdf

_______ Growth of Naval Power in the Indian Ocean: Dynamics and Transformation *Monograph Series*, National Maritime Foundation, New Delhi, January 2016 accessed at http://www.maritimeindia.org/View%20Profile/Growth%20of%20Naval.pdf

Sailo, Laldinkima (2012) Northeast India-Southeast Asia: Barrier to Bridge, *ISAS Working Paper No. 162* (Singapore: Institute of South Asian Studies) accessed at https://www.files.ethz.ch/isn/155422/ISAS_Working_Paper_162_-_Northeast_India-Southeast_Asia_20112012124917.pdf

Sakhuja, Vijay, and Gurpreet Khuranna, "India-Singapore Defence Cooperation: Exploring Strategic and Functional Compatibilities," in *The Merlion and the Ashoka Singapore–India Strategic Ties*, Anit Mukherjee, (ed.), Singapore: World Scientific, 2015.

SENZ, Anja & REINHARDT, Dieter (eds.) (2014) India, China and Southeast Asia – New Socio-Economic Developments Duisburger Arbeitspapiere Stasienwissenschaften Duisburg Working Papers on East Asian Studies No. 97, 2014 Anja SENZ, Dieter REINHARDT (eds.) Task Force: Connecting India, China and Southeast Asia – New Socio-Economic Developments accessed at https://www.uni-due.de/in-east_former_website/fileadmin/publications/gruen/paper97-2014.pdf

Scott, David, 2013. "India's Aspirations and Strategy for the Indian Ocean – Securing the Waves? *Journal of Strategic Studies*, DOI:10.1080/01402390.2012.728134

Shambaugh, David, "A Big Step Forward in U.S.-China Relations", accessed online on July 19, 2013 at http://www.chinausfocus.com/foreign-policy/a-big-step-forward-in-u-s-china-relations/.

Singh, Abhijit, 'An Indian Maritime Strategy for an Era of Geopolitical Uncertainty', *Journal of Defence Studies*, 9 (4), October-December 2015, pp. 7-19; URL http://idsa.in/jds/9_4_2015_AnIndianMaritimeStrategy

________ "Rebalancing India's Maritime Posture in the Indo-Pacific," 5 September 2014 accessed on October 2015 at http://thediplomat.com/2014/09/rebalancing-indias-maritime-posture-in-the-indo-pacific/

________ "The Indian Navy's New 'Expeditionary' Outlook", *ORF Occasional Paper # 37*, October 2012., New Delhi: Observer Research Foundation. accessed on 10 October at http://orfonline.org/cms/export/orfonline/modules/occasionalpaper/attachments/occasional_37_1351144676325.pdf

Singh, Bilveer, *The Vulnerability of Small States Revisited: A Study of Singapore's Post-Cold War Foreign Policy*. Yogyakarta, Indonesia: Gadjah Mada University Press, 1999.

________ "The Rise of Singapore-India Defense Relations in the Post-Cold War Era: Strategic and Security Implications," *Journal of International Studies*, Vol. 4, Kuala Lumpur: Universiti Utara Malaysia, 2008; accessed on 24 October 2015 at www.jis.uum.edu.my/images/pdf/4jis/3therise.pdf

________ "Southeast Asia-India Defence Relations in the Changing Regional Security Landscape," IDSA Monograph Series No. 4, May 2011, New Delhi: IDSA accessed at 23 October 2015 at http://www.idsa.in/system/files/MonographNo4.pdf

________ "Singapore-India Defence Relations amidst Changing Security Architecture in the Asia-Pacific" in *The Merlion and the Ashoka Singapore–India Strategic Ties*, Anit Mukherjee (ed.), Singapore: World Scientific, 2015.

Singh, Sinderpal and Syeda Sana Rahman, "The Next Stage of Singapore-India Relations: Possibilities and Prospects," *ISAS Working Paper* No: 91, 24 September 2009, accessed on 2 November 2015 at www.isn.ethz.ch/Digital-Library/Publications/Detail/?lang=en&id.

________ 2010. 'India-Singapore Relations: Constructing a 'New' Bilateral Relationship', *Contemporary Southeast Asia*, 32 (1), April 2010, pp. 70-97; accessed 28 October 2015 at http://www.jstor.org/stable/41288804

Tan, Seng, and Amitav Acharya, *Bandung Revisited: The Legacy of the 1955 Asian-African Conference for International Order,* Singapore: NUS Press, 2008.

Tellis, Ashley J. and Sean Mirski, *Crux of Asia: China, India and the Emerging World Order.* Washington D.C.: Carnegie Endowment for International Peace, 2013; accessed 4 November 2015 at http://carnegieendowment.org/files/crux_of_asia.pdf

Ting, Ming Hwa, 'Singapore-India Relations: A Return to History', *Austrian Journal of Southeast Asian Studies,* 2 (2), December 2009, pp. 122–44; accessed 2 November 2015 at: http://www.seas.at/aseas/2_2/pdf/ASEAS_2_2_A7.pdf

Toh, Mun-Heng, "ASEAN+6 as a Step Towards an Asian Economic Community," accessed on 27 October 2015 at http://www.eastasiaforum.org/2009/05/15/asean6-as-a-step-towards-an-asian-economic-community/

Vuwing, Alexander L., 'The Future of China's Rise: How China's Economic Growth Will Shift the Sino-U.S. Balance of Power, 2010–2040', *Asian Politics & Policy,* 4(3), 2012, pp. 401–23.

Zou, David Vumlallian and Kumar, Satish, M., 'Mapping a Colonial Borderland: Objectifying the Geo-Body of India's Northeast', *The Journal of Asian Studies,* 70 (1), February 2011, pp. 141–170. © The Association for Asian Studies, Inc., doi:10.1017/S0021911810002986

3

Act East Policy, Transactions Costs and Development of the North-East

Bhagirathi Panda

I. Introduction

India's Look East Policy, which was subsequently rephrased as Act East Policy finds its formal manifestation in 1992 against the backdrop of a number developments at the global, regional and national levels. At the global level, the cold war regime had come to an end. The eventual disintegration of the erstwhile USSR had its obvious economic and military implications for India. China was emerging as a global as well as regional economic and military power. The economies of China and Southeast Asia were growing at a much faster face compared to India. Our regional economic arrangement at our immediate neighbourhood, i.e. SAARC was a virtual non-starter, whereas, ASEAN was emerging as a powerful regional trade block and economic body. At home our balance of payment situation was fragile and our economy was too inward looking compared to small countries like Malaysia, Thailand, Singapore or Indonesia in Southeast Asia. Post-independence, our four decades of economic and strategic disengagement with countries of the Southeast Asia, has drifted us away from them in terms of realising any meaningful economic gains. Our belief that those olden days of cultural linkage with them would stand forever and find an auto convergence in realising economic dividends, proved unworkable.

It is against this background, forethought dawned on us to undertake this initiative called 'Look East Policy' (LEP) and use it to reach out to our Southeast Asian neighbours. This initiative was based on both strategic as well as developmental rationales. The strategic prudence was to get integrated with our Southeast Asian neighbours and ASEAN so as to counterbalance the growing Chinese dominance in Southeast Asia. It was also meant to assert our role in the Asian Region as a regional power, look beyond SAARC and possibly to establish our claim as an emerging global power. The countries of Southeast Asia particularly Singapore, Malaysia and Thailand were also jittery of the Chinese expansionist attitude and therefore wanted to balance it out by establishing increased strategic and economic relationship with India. Thus it was a felt mutual imperative for both India and countries of Southeast Asia. The economic rationale was based on the need to end our inward looking economy tag, look outward in terms trade, investment and flow of capital, and overcome in a sustained way our impending balance of payment crisis.

II. LEP and the Country: A Snapshot

The implementation of LEP and its consequent strategic and economic dividends for the country has accrued under two phases. The first phase of the policy was from 1992 to 2002 and the second phase started from 2003. However, in this write up we present brief overall benefits in different spheres from the beginning to the recent period of the implementation of this policy. In terms of improving strategic relations, during the period, i.e. 1992 and 2015, India has become a summit level partner of ASEAN and a member of the East Asian Summit. With respect to ASEAN, the value of

India's merchandise trade has expanded from US$ 2.9 billion in 1993 to US$58.7 billion in 2015. The volume of India's exports to ASEAN increased to US$ 25.20 billion in 2015–16 from a modest amount of US$ 10.41 billion in 2005–06. During the same period, India's imports from ASEAN experienced a phenomenal rise to the level of US $ 39.84 billion from a meagre amount of US$ 10.81 billion. Expressed in terms of compound annual growth rate (CAGR), India's exports to ASEAN over this period was of 9.2 per cent and its imports from ASEAN was of 14 per cent. For India in 2015–16, imports from ASEAN constituted about 10.5% of its total imports and exports to ASEAN constituted about 9.2% of its total exports. Foreign Direct Investments (FDI) from India to ASEAN has increased significantly by 98 per cent from US$606 million in 2014 to US$1.2 billion in 2015. Similarly, FDI flows from ASEAN to India has increased from US$1580 million in 2010–11 to US$5356 million in 2014–15. In terms of share in total FDI flows to India, FDI flows from ASEAN is up from 10.6% in 2010–11 to 21.6% in 2014–15.

The ASEAN–India Trade in Goods Agreement (AITIGA), signed on 13 August 2009 is a milestone in the history of free trade pacts as this has become one of the world's largest free trade areas (FTA) with almost 1.8 billion people and a combined GDP of US$4.5 trillion. Bilateral trade between India and CMLV countries has increased from a meagre $460 million in 2000 to $11.85 billion in 2014. The ASEAN-India Investment and Services Agreement came into force on 1st July 2015 and it holds a promise in the expansion of trade in services between the two regions. Tourism is another area that has seen significant expansion. Total number of tourists from the ASEAN countries visiting India during 2014 was 6,85,805. Similarly total no of tourists from India visiting ASEAN countries was 29,83,154.

III. AEP and North-East India

The above snapshot makes it clear that the LEP and its current reincarnation the AEP has brought in tangible economic and strategic benefits to the country. However, at the end of the phase-I of the policy, it was realised that the North Eastern Region (NER) has been sidestepped in terms of tangible benefits, although this region was in the proximity of Southeast and East Asian countries. It was felt by Government of India that without dovetailing the NER of India with Southeast and East Asia, such visualised economic and strategic integration under AEP would be incomplete, sun-optimal and unsustainable. Further, with the publication of the vision document 2020, it was formally acknowledged that the partition of the country and its perceived security dimension, had adversely affected the economic morale of the region. The region for almost six and half decades experienced cascading developmental crisis with the experimentation of an insular development model that overtly and covertly promoted the culture of rent seeking in the space and practice of development. The region was in dire need of an alternative development thinking and strategy to undo the damages inflicted on the region and its people by such myopic and selfish development model. It is against such a backdrop, it was felt prudent to consider AEP as an opportunity and position it as the alternative focal strategy of development of the region. Concomitantly, Government of India, particularly MEA went in to a proclamation mode inviting debate and engagement with important stakeholders of development including the wider civil society in the region. This more than one decade long proclamation and engagement has created some amount of eagerness and anxiety in equal proportions in the minds of general public with respect to the proclaimed benefits of the policy. While the policy gets its support from the echelons of government and a section of academia, there are sizeable sections in academia and civil society who too voice serious concerns. In its evolving state, this policy has implications for the region, in terms of trade, services, investment, tourism, migration, livelihood and employment, cultural exchange, security and above all rights of the indigenous people over resources and environment. At present, a lot of uncertainties exist with respect to the probable impacts of the implementation of the policy with respect to many of these variables.

In this paper we make a modest attempt, with the help of established concepts in economics and some available data, to bring some clarity with respect to the focal implementation of the policy. The paper is presented in sections. The introductory section, provides a brief on the genesis of the LEP, followed by a succinct description of the economic gains from it for the country as a whole in Section II. Section III reasons out the relevance of the policy for the NER. Section IV mentions the important strengths and challenges of the economy of the region and Section V outlines the progress of this policy particularly in the field of merchandise trade against this backdrop. Section VI provides a perceived framework of sequential process of success of AEP, followed by a discussion on 'transaction cost theory' in Section VII. Section VIII, builds a theoretical construction of the transactions costs approach linking it with the implementation of AEP in an environment of economic efficiency in NER. The concluding Section IX arrives at some insightful conclusions based on the main analysis and provides for some critical suggestions as a way forward.

IV. The NER Economy: Its Strength and Challenges

Having decided to use the AEP as the core strategy of development for the North Eastern Region, the criteria on which its success can be measured essentially would be its realisations in the front of strategic and economic benefits. In this paper, we only explain economic benefits as they are the ones which relatively matter more. These economic realisations, further, are to be prioritised on the basis of their immediacy and relevance for the people and the region. The NER economy has its own strengths. Some of its visible strengths are, (i) High Human Development Index (HDI) vis-a-vis the country(the HDI of the region as per the latest data for year 2007–08 stood at 0.573 as against the country's average of 0.513, (ii) perceived low labour costs because of high youth unemployment rate, (iii) availability of considerable size of English speaking people, (iv) endowment of natural resources including forests and hydro power potential, (v) strong community base (this has implication to reduce the information asymmetry and transaction costs), (vi) continuous improvement in economic and social infrastructures tending to match the national average and (vii) a tourists' paradise being the home to wild and elemental nature.

However, The NER economy also faces multiple economic challenges. Some of the important manifestations of these challenges are: (i) high youth unemployment rate (Overall youth unemployment rate in 2011–12 in the NER was 6.15 percent as against the national average of 4%. Urban female youth unemployment rate in NER was 16.18 per cent as against the Indian average of 11.7 percent), (ii) jobless growth (overall employment growth in NER has almost remained stagnant at 0.13 per cent during 2005 to 2012, D'souza, 2014), (iii) increased casualisation of women's employment (Lahoti and Swaminathan, 2013), (iv) distressed diversification of employment (Panda, 2011), (v) skewed structural transformation in income space (insignificant industrialisation and its contribution to regional domestic product) and (vi) less inter-state integrated economy in terms of infrastructure, production, exchange and marketing.

V. The Economic Gains for the Region under LEP and AEP Regime

It is against these strengths and challenges discussed in the above section, expanded trade in goods and services with countries of

Southeast Asia and East Asia including Bangladesh is being suggested (and rightly so) as one of the most important components of realising success under this policy. However, when we analyse the growth and magnitude of trade of this region with these countries (except Bangladesh), there is not much to cheer. This region shares borders with five countries such as Myanmar, Bhutan, Bangladesh, Nepal and China. Among all these countries, Myanmar stands out in terms of its strategic location as a gateway to the rest of the Southeast and East Asian countries. Both India and Myanmar share a common boarder stretching up to 1643 kms. Four states of NER, viz. Arunachal Pradesh, Manipur, Mizoram, and Nagaland share that international boarder. At present there are four Land Customs Stations (LCSs), viz. Moreh (Manipur), Zokhawthar (Mizoram), Nampong (Arunachal Pradesh), Avangkhu (Nagaland) through which formal boarder trade takes place between the NER and Myanmar. Trade through the last three LCSs virtually a non-starter. It is only through the Moreh LCS that more than 98% of the overland trade takes place.

An assessment of the trade situation between Myanmar and NER shows the insignificance of the volume of boarder trade between the NER and Myanmar (Table 1). NER's exports to Myanmar expressed as a percentage of the total Indian exports to Myanmar during the period 2006–07 to 2012–13 has consistently remained below 3%. Similarly during this period, NER's imports from Myanmar expressed as a percentage of the total Indian imports from Myanmar has remained below 2% except for the year 2012–13 where it has marginally crossed this mark. This explains the fact that NER as a region having such a huge international border with Myanmar has not been able to leverage the AEP for increased overland trade with Myanmar. Further, the trade deficit between this region and Myanmar has always been negative. An interesting development in the form of increased volume of trade is noticed for the year 2012–13 and 2013–14. The average import of NER from Myanmar for the period 2005–06 to 2011–12 was US$ 9.09 millions. This has increased by more than three times in 2013–14. Similarly, the average export from NER to Myanmar during the same period has also increased by more than 3 times in 2013–14. However, along with this increase in imports and exports, the trade deficit of NER with Myanmar has also increased as is evident from the figures of 2012–13 and 2014–15 (Table 2). Further, when one looks at the major commodities (Table 3) that have been exported from the NER to Myanmar in 2012–13 through boarder trade in Moreh, none of these commodities are having production base in the region. This implies that trade between NER and Myanmar from the NER point of view has been basically transit trade. Its exports are not based on the resources and product base of NER. Similarly its imports also do not confirm to the resource-industry linkage between the region and Myanmar.

Table 1: NER's Trade with Myanmar (US$ million)

Year	Indian Export to Myanmar	Indian Import from Myanmar	NER Export to Myanmar	NER Import from Myanmar	NER Share as a % of India	
					Exports	Imports
2005–06	132.72	718.40	4.13	11.28	3.11	1.57
2006–07	174.02	802.79	4.75	11.02	2.72	1.37
2007–08	212.23	893.52	3.92	10.91	1.84	1.22
2008–09	209.78	1195.26	4.43	5.49	2.11	0.45
2009–10	207.97	1289.80	5.95	7.79	2.86	0.60
2010–11	320.62	1017.67	4.50	8.30	1.40	0.82
2011–12	545.38	1381.15	6.54	8.87	1.20	0.64
2012–13	544.66	1412.69	11.67	26.96	2.14	1.91
2013–14	787.01	1395.67	17.71	30.92	2.25	2.22

*Source:*http://www.indiaembassyyangon.net/index.php?option=com_content&view=category&layout=blog&id=21&Itemid=122&lang=en

Table 2: India and NER's Trade Balance with Myanmar (US$ million)

Year	Indian Export to Myanmar	Indian Import from Myanmar	India's Trade Balance	NER Export to Myanmar	NER Import from Myanmar	NER's Trade Balance
2005–06	132.72	718.40	-585.68	4.13	11.28	-7.15
2006–07	174.02	802.79	-628.77	4.75	11.02	-6.27
2007–08	212.23	893.52	-681.29	3.92	10.91	-6.99
2008–09	209.78	1195.26	-985.48	4.43	5.49	-1.06
2009–10	207.97	1289.80	-1081.83	5.95	7.79	-1.84
2010–11	320.62	1017.67	-697.05	4.50	8.30	-3.80
2011–12	545.38	1381.15	-835.77	6.54	8.87	-2.33
2012–13	544.66	1412.69	-868.03	11.67	26.96	-15.29
2013–14	787.01	1395.67	-608.66	17.71	30.92	-13.21

Author's calculation based on data of DGFT, GOI.

Table 3: NER's Trade with Myanmar in 2012-13

Name of LCS	Major Commodities Traded	
	Exports	Imports
Moreh	Cumin seed, cotton yarn, auto parts, soya bean meal, wheat flour and pharmaceuticals.	Betel nuts, dry ginger, green mung beans, black matpe beans, turmeric roots, resin and medicinal herbs

Source: De and Mazumdar, 2014.

VI. AEP and the Conceptualised Sequential Process for its Success

The success of the AEP in the NER can be visualised in two dimensions, i.e. strategic and economic. However, the strategic dimension provides the initial grounding. To some extent, that grounding has been realised in terms of growing cultural and international engagements of the region with the countries of South Asia. However, the ultimate challenge is in the front of realising economic dividends. To realise economic dividends, first of all the policy and its imperatives should be acceptable to the people across the board in the region. Such an acceptance is dependent on, *inter alia*, linking it up with the expansion in the livelihood and employment opportunities of its people particularly the youth.

Expansion in livelihood and employment opportunities depends on emergence of a strong regional economic base led by networked fragmented industry and high end services sector. This eventually depends on reducing the present level of high transaction costs endemic in the region in pursuing investment and production activities. Therefore, the success of AEP noticeably, at the core, depends on the extent and rate of reduction in transaction costs. Figure 1 below shows such a sequential process.

Figure 1: The Conceptualised Sequential Process of Success of AEP

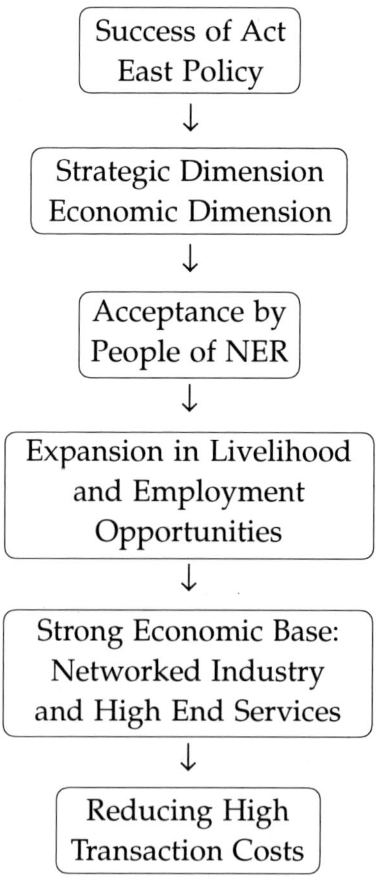

VII. Transaction Costs

Transaction costs as a concept owes its systematic origin in the works of Ronald Coase (1937, 1960), although in his first work 'The nature of the firm', he did not explicitly mention about it. Coase discussed it in the context of efficiency of firm in relation to market transactions with a number of examples. His transactions cost basically includes three types of costs: (i) search and information costs, (ii) bargaining and decision costs (i.e. negotiation and contract closure) and (iii) policing and enforcement costs. This concept of transaction costs was further analysed by Coase in the property rights framework when he published *The Problem Social Cost* in 1960. It is in this publication that Coase clearly establishes the link between transaction costs and property rights. However, it was Cheung (1969), who made use of this concept and made it specific and contextual to contracts and its choice. Subsequently Williamson (1975, 1985) technically expanded Coase's concept of transaction costs by bringing in the costs arising from inefficiencies in the selection of the adequate institutional arrangement of a firm. It essentially means comparison between different modes of contracting under different institutional arrangements. This view of Williamsons better known as the traditional transactions cost economics (TCE) could provide an explanation to the situations which were earlier considered by the Neo-classicals as atypical contracting practices and industrial structures. However, Williamson's analysis of the scope of transaction costs was subsequently felt to be limited and inadequate particularly with respect to the developing countries situations. In these countries, the macro institutional environment always impacts the transactions costs by impacting the micro intuitional arrangements of the traditional TCE approach of Williamsons and the three important dimensions of this TCE, i.e. asset specificity, uncertainty and frequency. This takes us to North's approach to transaction costs. North (1990), puts the transaction cost analysis in the framework of economics of development by linking it with the complex institutional structure of developing countries. He explains that transaction costs are affected by the formal and informal institutions as well as organisations of a society. Institutions to him are the rules of the game and organisations are the mechanisms through which these rules are created, enforced and confirmed. Institutions can play a positive role in controlling uncertainty and they can also play a negative role in increasing transaction costs. He explains how powerful firms/industries/ organisations can also create institutions to promote their self-interests by creating an environment of institution lock-in and path dependency. To sum up, with addition of North's institutional approach, the transaction cost analysis propounded by Coase and Williamson has become a very dynamic model to explain the state and process of underdevelopment in developing countries in general and the efficiency status of firms, industries in the field of production and trade in particular. As explained in the previous section, the success of the AEP depends to a great extent on the reduction of this transaction costs and as evidenced at present, there exists huge transaction costs in the economy of NER that prevent economic efficiency to be realised, networked industrial centres to come up and trade competitiveness to be obtained. With this theoretical framework in mind, we move to the subsequent section to throw some light on the nature of such transaction costs in the NER.

VIII. Transaction Costs, Economic Efficiency, AEP and the NER

It is a fact that some visible improvements have happened in the front of infrastructure and industrialisation post-2000 in the NER. Road, railway, water transportation, telecommunication facilities have all relatively improved across the states in the region. However, the region comparatively lags the country when it comes to infrastructures like railways, power and inland water transportation. Other areas where it does poorly are in the fields of logistics and trade facilitation. Trade cost incidence to NER is very high compared to other developing countries (De and Mazumdar, 2014). Although, road infrastructure has fast increased in the region, but quality of the roads and their maintenance is a matter of concern. Having better connectivity is important. However, what is now more challenging for the success of AEP is the efficiency with which the region makes use of this critical connectivity. As mentioned earlier, existence of high transaction costs in the NER is the most important stumbling block in the front of realising networked production centres and economic efficiency. Figure 2 makes a list of such components of transaction costs in the framework of transaction cost analysis of Coase, Williamsons and North discussed in section 7.

One of the important visible components of transactions costs in NER is the issue of property rights. A relevant area where this issue comes up poignantly is the tradability of land and its acquisition for construction of infrastructure and establishment of firms and industries. There are issues with respect to its ownership and tradability which have their origins in the societal norms of different regions of the region. Here we find a criss-cross between Coase's version of transactions costs and North's version of transaction costs. Apparently manifestation of a Coase-type transaction cost has its origin and continuity in the institutional plane that North so explicitly explains. This has a Williamson angle in it too and that is all about choosing and continuing with a societal governance structure for vested interests. To give some concrete local examples, IOC Ltd. wants to set up a bottling plant in and around Shilling area but it is finding it difficult to acquire the required land. Expansion of Guwahati-Shillong National Highway was held up for a considerable period for non-acquisition of land from the residents. Even as on today, a patch of 5 kms of the NH is yet to be fourlaned because of non-acquisition of land from the owners. Further, expansion of Shillong Airport and particularly its runway is also marred with such problems of land

Figure: 2. Transactions Cost in NER

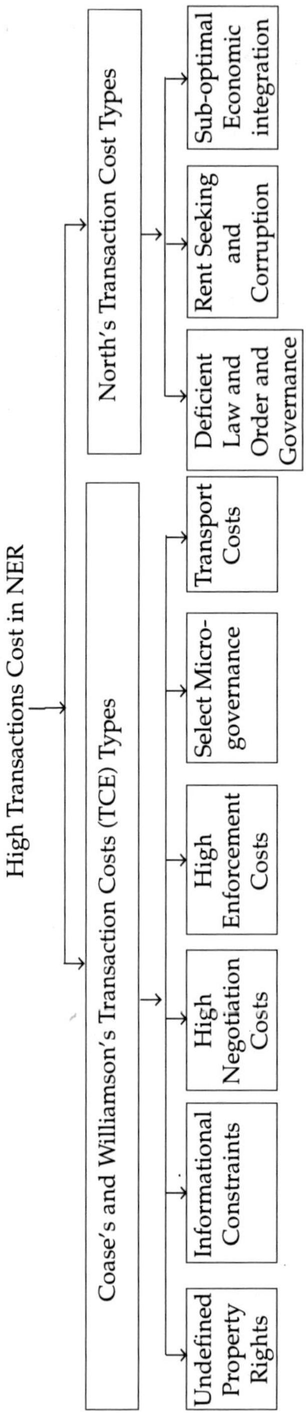

acquisition. Many a young entrepreneurs find it difficult to start their enterprise because of land acquisition/procurement problems.

The next component is the negotiation and enforcement costs. Negotiation becomes costly because of presence of multiple stakeholders. Let us take the case of cross-border trade in Moreh in Manipur. At the firm level implementation of any policy becomes costly and sometimes difficult because it involves engagements with the state government, insurgent and underground elements, the Indian Army, relevant central institutions, etc. In many states, there are multiple formal and informal authorities having their respective rules, norms and stipulations on acquiring properties, getting license, doing business, etc. You have to negotiate with the central government, state government, autonomous district councils (ADCs, where they exist), local traditional institutions, underground elements, extortionists, etc. Similarly, the existence of such multiple stakeholders, formal rules and informal norms and practices and the non-existence of an independent judiciary in few states at the district and sub-district levels make the cost of enforcement of contract very high.

Another Williamsonian component of transaction cost is the arrangement of working under a constrained micro-governance structure. The earlier case of working under the dual exchange rate with respect to boarder trade at Moreh was such a classic example. The official currency exchange rate of Myanmar was highly overvalued, whereas there was an unofficial market determined rate which was more realistic. This situation encouraged exporters from India to avail the unofficial channel of informal trade. This had also another dampening impact on the incentive of banks to operate at Moreh as they used to lose their opportunity to deal in foreign exchange and earn commissions. The situation has now, of course improved, with the economic reforms in 2012 in Myanmar. One more factor that increases the transaction cost is the high transportation cost because of poor connectivity, bad condition of the roads, frequent bandhs and road blockades in Manipur and other parts of NER. For example, as per a statement made by the then Chief Minister of Manipur in the Manipur assembly on July 2010, the state witnessed 628 bandhs and blockades during the 15 year period from 1995 to June 2010 with a combined loss of Rs. 2828 crore to the state exchequer. As per an estimate of the Department of Economics, Manipur University, during the infamous 120 days prolonged bandh and economic blockade of NH 2 and NH 37 in 2011, Manipur suffered a loss of Rs. 245.64 crore at a rate of Rs. 2.67 crore per day.

Finally, let us have a look on the prevalence of North's specified transaction costs, which basically arise because of macro-institutional factors. One of the important macro institutional variables that affect transaction cost in the region is deficient law and order situation and governance. This is reflected as mentioned earlier in frequent bandhs and blockades, extortions, smuggling across borders, collection of illegal fees and lack of effective mechanism to resolve conflicts, etc. Rent seeking and corruption are two other North specified macro institutional variables that have significant implications in terms of increased transaction costs. Rent seeking is basically to employ any individual or organisation's office and resources to get some economic gain without contributing directly to the society in terms of actual wealth creation. This therefore includes, all kinds of bribery, lobbying, intimidation, pressure tactics used by individuals, groups or organisations including Government to exploit its resources/position to gain some economic benefits/resources without contributing to direct production of goods and services. Rent seeking in different forms is widespread in the NER. All kinds of bribery at different levels of government, extortions by individuals, groups and organisations by exercise of their position and powers through explicit or implicit coercion and threat have contributed to this rent seeking culture and in the process have increased the transaction cost of undertaking productive activities as an entrepreneur. As Murphy, Shleifer and Vishny (1991) mentioned, 'In situations where the gains from rent-seeking or predation are greater than the returns of production, entrepreneurial talent is more likely to engage in rent-seeking and corruption. To reiterate, this is more likely in societies with poor governance, and where there is more to loot due to the presence of natural resource revenues, privatized enterprises, or where great transformation is in train. In countries where more talents are allocated to rent-seeking rather than production, growth and regulatory failure will eventually ensue.' Post-partition, when a patron-client type of development model was unleashed in this part of the country, rent seeking gradually emerged and got consolidated over the last seven decades. This has largely killed the native entrepreneurial urge for undertaking productive activities by increasing the transaction cost.

Last but not the least, NER is yet to emerge as an integrated economic and governance entity. Although the states were created here on ethnic and political lines, today the developmental imperatives require that they have to emerge as a single economic entity. Working of firms and economic agents under such a sub-optimal regional economic arrangement increases the transaction cost. Agents can significantly reduce their transportation costs and realise more of vertical production integration if intra-regional physical and governance communications gets considerably improved. This kind of integration would lead to reduction in market-related transaction costs including the costs of negotiation and enforcement of contracts. For example, efficiency in export and import of commodities and services requires critical scale of production and demand respectively. Many times individual states on their own are not able to realise it, but they can do it if they come together.

IX. Concluding Remarks

The objective of dovetailing of the AEP with the development strategy for the NER under the initiative of AEP, although is a late realisation by Government of India, is very relevant to NER at the present juncture. However, as on the day, there exists huge gap between the relevance and potential economic benefits of the policy and its actualisation. Given the institutional and socio-cultural arrangements in the north eastern society, the success of this kind of an approach for the NER depends on the acceptability of this policy and its attributes and overtones by the people at large. This, going by the demographic profile of the region, largely depends on the scope to expand the livelihood and employment opportunities for the youth without essentially changing the core cultural, environmental and societal values of the people and community. The most desired means of realising such an expansion in employment opportunities would be by way of expansion in trade, investment and services activities with the Southeast Asia and Bangladesh. This to happen depends on development of appropriate fragmented production of goods and services networks in the region. This again requires finding out complementaries in the field of production of goods and services between NER and Myanmar. Currently, the scope of having such networked and fragmented production centres is plausible in industries like (a) pharmaceuticals including herbal products, (b) bamboo and wood products, (c) cement, (d) agro-processing, (e) textiles, (f) refined petroleum products, (g) other non-metallic mineral products, (h) rubber products and (i) horticulture. Electronics, handlooms and handicrafts and leather products also are potential products around which production networks can also come up. In the front of services: (a) tourism, (b) health, (c) medical, (d) education and (e) transportation are the identified services which have the potential for development through the fragmented networks approach. These envisaged production centres are required to be adequately serviced with all kinds of connecting and in-place infrastructures like roads, railway lines, air services, inland water transportation, uninterrupted power supply, Internet and telecommunication services, efficient manpower , adequate hospitality and recreation centres, efficient governance including law and order, etc. so as to reduce on transportation and transaction costs and facilitate production of goods and different types of services including tourism, education, health, banking and insurance. At the present juncture, the ground situation in NER is that it has not been able develop such visible fragmented production centres and network them in terms of communications and infrastructure because of existence of high transaction costs of both North and Williamson types. Our argument in this paper is that without reducing substantially the prevalent high transaction costs in the region, we cannot make any headway. Government of India has already promoted the required critical strategic integration through a number of regional and multilateral collaborations and institutional reforms such as FTA with ASEAN, transnational physical connectivity through construction of roads and rail links, strengthening Indo–BIMSTEC, Indo–ASEAN, and Indo–BMIC relationships. However, the subsequent relevance, scaling up, continuity and sustainability of this policy and its dovetailing with the development requirements of NER depends on how quickly and efficiently we reduce on the all-pervasive high transaction costs. This requires, *inter-alia,* (i) an impetus to social entrepreneurship. Social entrepreneurship as a practice can be leveraged to reduce this high transaction costs particularly through social innovations which can make the property right regime, and negotiation and enforcement of contracts arrangements certain, (ii) a critical calibrated convergence in the establishment space in development and to be specific, across the four important components therein, i.e. the government, the market, the community and the civil society. Presently, the establishment space in development in NER exhibits disproportionate parallelism. This parallelism (which is nothing but the manifestation of the macro-institutions of North) causes disconnect, creates unwanted conflicts and takes away the potential complementariness across the different establishments which is critical to the endeavour of reducing the high transaction costs and the ultimate success of the Act East Policy in NER.

REFERENCES

ASSOCHAM, *India-ASEAN Trade and Investment Relations: Opportunities and Challenges*, New Delhi, 2016.

Coase, R., 'On The Nature of the Firm', *Economica*, 4, 1937, pp. 386–405.

De and Mazumdar, *Developing Cross-Border Production Networks between North Eastern Region of India, Bangladesh and Myanmar: A Preliminary Assessment*. RIS, New Delhi, 2014.

De, Prabir and Amrita Saha, "Logistics, Trade and Production Networks: An Empirical Investigation". *RIS Discussion Paper No. 181*. Research and Information System for Developing Countries (RIS), New Delhi, 2013.

De, Prabir, 'Reassessing Transaction Costs of Trade at the India-Bangladesh Border', *Economic and Political Weekly*, 43 (29), 2008.

Murphy, Kevin, Abdrei Shleifer and Robert Vishny, 'Why is Rent-Seeking So Costly to Growth?' *American Economic Review*, 83(2), 1993, pp. 409–14.

NEC, *Northeastern Region: Vision 2020*. North Eastern Council (NEC), Ministry of Development of North Eastern Region, Shillong, 2007.

North, D. *Institutions, Institutional Change and Economic Performance*, Cambridge University Press, 1990.

Sharma, Atul, Mehta, Pradeep Kumar, *Exploring Indo-ASEAN Economic Partnership in Globalising World*, New Delhi: Bookwell, 2006.

Sharma, Atul, 'The North-East as a Gateway to Southeast Asia: Big Dream and Home Truths', *Man and Development*, June 2006, pp. 35–50.

Silvia Saravia and Michael Dietrich, *Emergence and impact of transaction costs in developing economies: the case of the Nicaraguan coffee industry during the Sandinista Regime (1979–1990)*, Sheffield: University of Sheffield, 2006.

Williamson, O.W. 1991, *The Nature of the Firm: Origins, Evolution, and Development*, New York: Oxford University Press New York, 1991.

4

Look North-East before Acting East:
Synergising North-East with Act East Policy*

C. Joshua Thomas

Look East Policy (LEP) was actually initiated in the wake of the Liberalisation, Privatisation and Globalisation (LPG) of the Indian economy in 1990. It was born out of conviction that South East Asia (SEA) is more important for India than the traditional western trading partners. In a sense, LEP is a strategic shift in India's foreign policy. However, the concrete shape was given to LEP only when the India-Myanmar border trade agreement was signed on January 31, 1994. From then on Public Diplomacy Division of the Ministry of External Affairs (MEA), the Ministry of Home Affairs, Ministry of Commerce and Industries and of course the Ministry of DoNER of the government of India has organised and sponsored scores of seminars, workshops and conferences on LEP. Scholars at the masters and the doctoral level in different universities of the North-Eastern region had done a large number of researches on LEP and the number of books published on LEP has been substantial in the last one decade. The ICSSR North Eastern Regional Centre had organized an international conference on "India's Look East Policy and the North Eastern Region:

Strengthening the Continental Route" on 21-22 March 2013 at Shillong. Looking into the available literature on LEP, we can say that under the LEP the North-Eastern Region was supposed to be developed with infrastructure of international standard, by way of superior connectivity through 3Rs+1A—road, rail and river and air connectivity. Now, LEP initiative has completed more than two decades, however, the ground reality is different. At the East Asia Summit (13th November 2014) held at the Myanmar's capital Nay Pyi Taw, Prime Minister Narendra Modi told the world leaders that his government has accorded high priority to turn India's erstwhile Look East Policy into an Act East Policy. Whether it is Look East Policy or Act East Policy, it cannot be successful unless North-East region finds its share in it. As someone has aptly said, "You can't look east unless you look at North-East". This article would like to articulate the location and space for NE region in the new dispensation of AEP integrating the region's economy with that of Bangladesh through better connectivity, which is not only viable and desirable but is crucial to its peace and prosperity and also success of LEP/AEP.

I

There are already a lot of analytical writings available on LEP/AEP, the goals and gains; its success and failures, etc. Scholars on India's foreign policy and North-East watchers tend to agree that LEP is a sound, most appropriate and well thought out policy that helps further India's geo-strategic and geo-economic interest in a very important theatre, Southeast and East Asia. For the last two decades, public leaders, academics and diplomats have been speaking and writing on LEP/AEP and its different aspects in great detail. Here I would like to make a few comments that would be based on my personal observation in the region for the last more than two decades, and also personally being in the ICSSR-NERC which has sponsored and organised several seminars, conferences related to border trade, LEP, etc. In most of the conferences, seminars and the available literature on LEP the scholars had highlighted the various dimensions of Look East Policy.

The North-Eastern region is the physical and cultural bridge between India, Southeast Asia and East Asia. The prosperity of NE depends a great deal on its contacts, and its relationship with the countries in the north, east and south of it, as the region is surrounded by Bangladesh, Bhutan, China, Nepal and Myanmar and shares borders with them too.. When we look at the LEP or AEP basically it has three important objectives: 1) To cultivate extensive economic and strategic relations with Southeast Asian nations in order to bolster India's standing as a regional power. It has its emphasis on connectivity, trade, investment and tourism to bring about a seamless integration of economic spaces, enabling maximum optimisation of human and resource potential between the two sides; 2) LEP is reinventing the North-East economy, which has been comparatively very poor. In a sense the LEP aims for the promotion and development of NE and aims at better connectivity and dependable transport connectivity; 3) To build bilateral and multilateral relations with the nations in ASEAN and East Asia.

In a nutshell we can say that LEP has both geo-economic and geo-political objectives in Southeast and East Asia with a keen desire to develop its North-Eastern region.

Moreover, we may say that the LEP has three components or interests: the national interest, the regional interest and the local interest. The national interest focuses on the peace and prosperity of the nation and the establishment of better relations with her neighbours. The regional interest directs on the development of the North-East as its priority. And in the local interest the benefit of LEP must percolate down to the village level in the region. In a sense, the potential of India's LEP is a new paradigm of development in the North-East development perspective.

Rajiv Sikri, a seasoned Indian diplomat has rightly pointed out that the Look East Policy, "envisages the region not as the periphery of India, but as the centre of thriving and integrated economic space linking two dynamic regions with a network of highways, railways, pipelines, transmission lines crisscrossing the region."[1] Thus, the states in the North-East are expected to play a stellar role in the LEP and be a prime beneficiary. Ambassador Alok Sen said, "Located in the cusp of South and Southeast Asia it appears that North-East states have been intended by geography to play this vital role"[2] In China, the underdeveloped Yunnan province of South West China under its Gate Way Policy or South Asia economic policy is the main instrument for doing business with neighbouring countries such as Myanmar, Laos and Vietnam. Yunnan was historically underdeveloped, geographically isolated and economically backward about two decades ago. But, when we look at China, first large investments were made in Yunnan to equip it to play the role of bridge head. As a result the Yunnan province has been lifted to a higher place of prosperity. Similarly the LEP was expected to do the same for the states in the North-Eastern region. However, when we look at the performance of the two decades old LEP, the states in the NER did not reap the benefit of the policy, whereas, the regions which have sea access reaped the full benefit of LEP. In this regard we need to look at the peculiarity of NER which has been discussed by several research studies and report and some are:

- Nature of physical terrain - Long pourous international border with Bangladesh, Bhutan, China and Myanmar.
- Poor infrastructure and economic base
- Weak communication link
- Lack of capital investment
- Insurgency, extortion, violent conflict in the region
- High level of resource mismanagement
- Lack of coordinated policy between states in the region
- Basically the region is a production dependent economy

There is a feeling in the North-Eastern region that LEP could be successful unless India does not Look East through the Northeast. If we overlook North-East then it will have very little meaning to the region and to the people of the region. Now, the main question is how to synergise North-East with the Look East or Act East Policy?

In this regard there is a need to articulate on the location of and space for North-East within the Act East Policy and for this we need to emphasise on two investments: 1) Hard power investment; 2) Soft power investment.

Hard Power Investments

1. Focus on infrastructure and connectivity—development is impossible without a good communication network of 3Rs: Road, Rail, River and 1-A, air connectivity. Massive investments are required in new areas and to upgrade the existing ones.
2. Focus on industrialisation[3]
3. Focus on issues identified in the Vision-2020 documents prepared by the North Eastern Council in collaboration with NIPFP for the Ministry of DoNER, Government of India.

There are a number of studies done by different agencies on the above mentioned aspects but my focus is on the soft power investment.

Soft Power Investment

It is time for the people in the North-East and the other states of the region to articulate their own priorities and preferences; we also need to reassess our strengths and establish its synergy with the Act East Policy. Ambassador Rajeev Bhatia in his address at the conference emphatically mentioned about "diplomacy for development." Taking a cue from his address, I would like to put forward four aspects of diplomacy for development of the region that can synergise North-East with Act East Policy:

1. Language Diplomacy[4] – NE has a good English-based education system and has the potential to impart English

education to the people in South East Asia and East Asian countries

2. Health Diplomacy – NE has a strong Medicare environment, it would be good to see the example set by the Shija hospital in Imphal in reaching out to the patients of Myanmar.
3. Cultural Diplomacy – the people of North-East has strong ethnic and cultural linkage with the people in the Southeast Asia and this can build people-to-people contact between North-East and Southeast Asia.
4. Tourism Diplomacy – Mr. M.P. Bez Barua has done excellent work on the tourism aspect, which can serve as a guideline to promote Act East Policy in favour of North-Eastern region tourism in bringing closer Southeast Asia to North-East India.

The above mentioned social capital and service-oriented economy should be recognised by the states in the region to synergise the AEP.

II

Both Bangladesh and Myanmar are the most important nations in the success of AEP as India shares a long border with both the countries. Therefore, the success of AEP will depend to a large extent on India's relations with Myanmar and Bangladesh and domestic situation in both countries.

With Bangladesh the region shares 2216 kms long border with four important states such as Assam, Meghalaya, Tripura and Mizoram border; on the other hand, with Myanmar, the North-Eastern region has 1643 kms and states such as Arunachal Pradesh, Nagaland, Manipur and Mizoram has porous border.

In Myanmar the problem exists on Highway nos. 39 and 53, wherein the law and order in the form of bandh, curfew, etc., is a great of cause of concern and this cripples the trade, transport and connectivity. The following data affirms that:

Year	No. of Dates bandh on both HW no 39 & 53[5]
2004-05	92 days
2005-06	121
2006-07	83
2007-08	103
2008-09	60
2009-10	154
2010-11	292
2011-12	90

The bandh and law and order problem in the Kohima-Imphal and Moreh-Tamu sector makes our trade and connectivity with Myanmar very poor and therefore we are not able to synergise the LEP/AEP in a productive way. Instead of Myanmar, one can say that synergising Bangladesh economy with that of the northeast of India would be far more realistic and beneficial to the region in India's Act East Policy.

It is often said, Bangladesh is India locked as NE is Bangladesh locked.[6] NE and Bangladesh together hold enormous promises for the benefit of AEP.

Improved North-East and Bangladesh connectivity will help to overcome the geographical, emotional and economic distance between the NE and the rest of India. The Kolkata-Guwahati distance will be halved and the distance between Kolkata and other places like, Agartala, Silchar, Aizawl, Shillong will be reduced to less than one-third.[7] Thus, integrating the region's economy with that of Bangladesh through better connectivity is not only viable and desirable but is crucial to the AEP and also to the peace and prosperity of the region.

At present Bangladesh is a rice and fish surplus country and it can meet the food security in the North-Eastern region and more particularly in the state of Meghalaya. According to a report prepared by the Meghalaya Veterinary Department in 2011-12:

Beef annual consumption in the state is 13,988 metric tons and the state could have on its own 5056 metric tons and there is a short age of 8,932 metric tons; pork 8,704 and the state could have on its own 7309 and there is a shortage 1,395 metric tons; and fish 11,000 metric tons and the state could have on its own 5048 metric tons and there is a shortage of 5,952. It is an open secret that cattle have been smuggled into Bangladesh thru more than 200 different illegal porous borders in to Bangladesh and if these cattle are retained in North-East it can meet our food security, or if it is made as a formal trade then the state will earn out of this trade.

The Federal government of India looks at the States in the North-East with and through "security prism". There is a great desire and strong demand from different sections in the North-Eastern region for the reopening of Stilwell Road.[8] However, the ministries like defence, external affairs and home affairs at New Delhi have a different opinion and they feel that opening of Stilwell Road will compromise with the security concern of the nation. Perhaps one should understand that it is not the opening of Stilwell Road that will be a threat to national security, rather poverty; lack of development; poor governance; and disparity in growth, the standard of living and the living condition may be the greatest threats to the national security. Therefore, we may say that the State needs to first establish food security before any other security. This food security can be established through connectivity with our neighbouring countries, particularly with Bangladesh and Myanmar. Ambassador V.S. Seshadri aptly said it is time to demonstrate an 'Act East' Policy[9] and now the ball is with the Union government to re-look and re-frame the erstwhile Look East Policy and make the States in the North-East region with adequate internal preparation by looking North-East before looking look east or act east policy.

REFERENCES

* An earlier version of this paper was presented at the national seminar on "Integrating North-East in India's Act East Policy" organised by the Indian Council of World Affairs (ICWA), New Delhi, held on 23 February 2015.

1. Rajiv Sikri's lecture 'North-East India and India's Look East Policy', in CENISEAS Forum 'Towards a New Asia: Transnationalism and North-East India'.

2. Alok Sen, 'Success and Failure of Look East Policy', talk delivered in international conference on 'India's Look East Policy and the North-Eastern Region: Strengthening the Continental Route', organised by the ICSSR North Eastern Regional Centre at the North Eastern Council, Shillong, on 21-22 March 2013.
3. Special Feature article on 'Industries in North-East', in *Eastern Panorama*, Guwahati, February 2015, pp.23-25.
4. Toki Blah, 'NAMO, the North-East and the Look East', *The Shillong Times*, 22 September 2014.
5. Subir Bhaumik, 'Look East Through Northeast': Challenges and Prospects for India, *ORF Occasional Paper* no. 51, June 2014, Observer Research Foundation, New Delhi, p.15.
6. R.N. Ravi, 'India's Look East Policy and North-East', *Assam Tribune*, Guwahati, January 13, 2013; also see, R.N. Ravi, 'BCIM Economic Corridor: A Blatant Hoax', *Assam Tribune*, 22 July 2014.
7. Gurudas Das and C. Joshua Thomas, *Report on Promotion of Cross Border Trade as a Strategy for Economic Development of the Frontier States in India's North-East*, Department of Economic Affairs, Ministry of Finance, Government of India, New Delhi, 2014.
8. C. Joshua Thomas, 'The Great Snake: Stilwell Road – A Panacea for the Development of India's North-East and the Deepening of India-China Bilateral Relations', paper presented at the conference on China-South Asia at the School of Development Studies, Yunnan University, Kunming, China, 4-5 April 2013.
9. V.S. Seshadri, 'Time to Demonstrate an Act East Policy', *The Hindu*, Chennai, 13 November 2014.

5

Reaping Dividend from India's Act East Policy:

What North-East Can Offer?

Ujjwal Kanti Paul and Gurudas Das

The end of the Cold War era with the collapse of Soviet Union in 1991 saw a swift global reconstruction. While United States of America became the most powerful country in the world, China emerged as the face of the East. Look East Policy was a course of correction in India's foreign policy to the changing global order. India established institutional linkages with the Association of South East Asian Nations (ASEAN) and its member countries to strengthen its bilateral relationship. Over the last two and half decades, the Look East Policy (LEP) and its successor Act East Policy (AEP) have helped India to reorient its trade and investment strategies from *West to East*. By 2011-14, ASEAN+3 member countries emerged as the largest trading partner of India occupying a share of nearly 23 percent of the total trade. During the same period, these countries became the second largest investor in India with 23.23 percent share of the total investment (Das et al., 2016). However, despite having a substantial reserve of natural resources, close cultural similarities and a contiguous land border of over 1700 km with Myanmar, an important ASEAN member, northeastern region of India (NER) could not reap much dividend from the LEP or AEP. Out of the eight states here, the per capita income of four states—Assam, Manipur, Meghalaya and Tripura—comprising nearly 90 percent of region's total population, lags behind the country's average income. Although, there is no unanimous opinion among the scholars that explains the failure of LEP in India's NER, bottlenecks in infrastructure are identified as one of the most significant blockade in the economic progress of the region.

Several cross-border connectivity projects such as India-Myanmar-Thailand highway, Trans-Asian railway network, Kaladan Multimodal Transport Project, etc., have been envisaged to overcome the infrastructural bottlenecks in the region. These logistical initiatives are likely to turn NER from an isolated landlocked peripheral territory to a land-linked territory integrated with the rapidly growing economies of the Southeast Asian region. However, connectivity might be necessary but not a sufficient condition for development. The rate of economic progress will depend on how efficiently the resources of the region are utilised and marketed leveraging the revamped connectivity. The current literature does not satisfactorily answer as to how will dyadic and triadic value chain linkages between NER and East and Southeast Asian countries be established? Which resources in NER can profitably be marketed to the ASEAN and its member countries? The present paper will discuss four prominent resources of the region showing the scope for their integration with the global value chain.

Pineapple

India is the sixth largest producer of pineapple in the world. During 2012-13, India produced 6.69 percent (1570 thousand MT) of world's total pineapple from over 10 percent (105 thousand Ha) of total land under pineapple cultivation. However, India's share in the global pineapple export market is less than 1 percent. This sharply contrasts the performance of other major pineapple producers in the world such as Costa Rica, Thailand and Philippines. For instance, Costa Rica—the largest pineapple producer in the world—enjoys nearly 40 percent share in the global pineapple export market from just 11 percent share in production.

NER produces more than 48 percent of India's total pineapple, albeit using nearly 70 percent of the total area under cultivation. The non-use of any chemical inputs is cited as one of the major factors behind low productivity of crops like pineapple in the region. Nevertheless, it brings a wonderful opportunity to market this perennial crop at a premium price to the increasingly growing health conscious customer segment that demands chemical-free food. However, in the absence of access to the developed market, currently, a large part of produce is either wasted at the orchard or sold in the local market at a very low price. As a result, growers have almost no incentive to invest in productivity enhancing resources.

The proposed IMT highway can be used to market these pineapples to Thailand, which is the world's largest exporter of pineapple juice (17.92 percent share). As Thailand inadvertently suffers due to the shortage of raw material in almost nine months in a year, securing access to a steady source of chemical-free pineapple will be a win-win proposition for both the countries. While the growers in the region will fetch higher price, the Thai marketers will be able to meet their production target. Small scale fruit processing units can be set up in major production regions through public-private partnership. These units can process the pineapples before exporting them to the Thai market. Obtaining organic certification will make the produce even more valuable. Table 1 highlights that pineapple traders in Cachar district of Assam can reap over 125 percent return on investment by exporting pineapples to the Thai market.

Figure 1: Share of Production and Export (%)

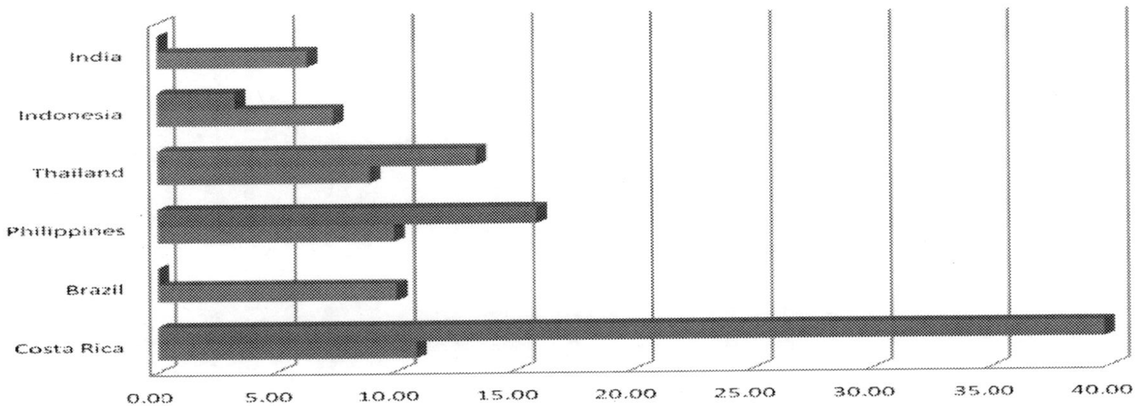

	Costa Rica	Brazil	Philippines	Thailand	Indonesia	India
Export	39.75	0.06	15.89	13.37	3.29	0.06
Production	10.84	10.02	9.92	8.92	7.41	6.34

Source: *FAOstat* (*http://www.fao.org/faostat/en/#data*), *Comtrade* (*http://comtrade.un.org/db/dqBasicQueryResults.aspx?px=H1&cc=091010&r=699&y=2015*)

Table 1: Approximate Cost and Profitability of Selling Pineapple at the Thai Market (via IMT Highway)

Sl.No.	Particulars	Amount
1	Current farm gate price (Rs/ton)	6035
2	Price at the secondary market (Rs/ton)	10000
3	Distance (km)	1400
4	Transportation cost (Rs 6/km/ton)	8400
5	Transit fee (Rs.5/ton/km)	7000
6	Wastage (20 percent)	2000
7	Miscellaneous (Rs/ton)	200
8	Total Cost (Rs/ton)	29000
9	Avg. wholesale price (Rs/ton)	60000
10	Margin (%)	106.89
11	Price after adjusting premium for organic production (20% of avg. wholesale price)	72000
12	Cost incurred for certification (10% of total cost)	2900
13	Margin after adjusting for premium and certification cost (%)	125.7

Source: Author's estimation.

Ginger

With 26.6 percent share in the total production, India is the largest ginger producer in the world followed by China (15.19 percent). However, its share in the global ginger export market is just 2.74 percent. China, on the other hand, has more than 52 percent share in the global ginger export market. A close observation of India's ginger trade discerns some peculiar trend. The largest proportion of India's ginger (35.61) goes to Bangladesh. However, Bangladesh pays the least price per kilogram of ginger. Whereas, Singapore, Thailand and Japan jointly receive less than 10 percent of India's total ginger despite paying the highest price per kilogram. This highlights the need for reorient India's ginger trade.

Nearly 57 percent of India's ginger is produced in NER. With 45 percent of region's total production, Assam is the largest ginger producing state in the region followed by Meghalaya (18 percent), Arunachal Pradesh (16 percent) and Nagaland (10 percent). NER can export the locally produced ginger either fresh or after processing them as biscuits, candy, juice, beer, etc., to the leading importing nations like Japan, Singapore, Thailand, etc. Moreover,

Figure 2: Share of Production and Export (%)

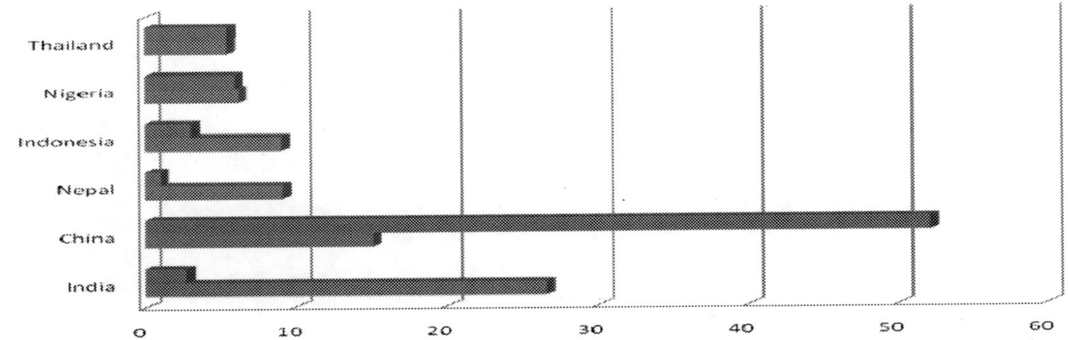

	India	China	Nepal	Indonesia	Nigeria	Thailand
Export	2.74	52.16	1.01	3.08	5.98	5.50
Production	26.6	15.19	9.15	9.06	6.23	5.45

Source: FAOstat (http://www.fao.org/faostat/en/#data), Comtrade (http://comtrade.un.org/db/dqBasicQueryResults.aspx?px=H1&cc=091010&r= 699&y=2015)

like pineapple, most of the ginger in the region is produced without applying any synthetic input. As a result, these ginger products can be sold at a premium price after using necessary organic certification.

Bamboo

With 25 percent of country's total forest cover, NER has gained worldwide attention for its diverse and extensive forest resources. Nearly 64 percent of the total area in the region is covered by forests (CFI 2006). Bamboo is one of the most significant constituents of the forest. Nearly 65 percent of global bamboo resources are available in the Asian province and with 30 percent of the global total; India has the largest bamboo resources in the world. Within the country, NER (40.11 percent) has the maximum bamboo resources followed by Madhya Pradesh (9.36 percent), Chhattisgarh (8.14 percent), and Maharashtra (8.21 percent). Despite having significant bamboo reserve, India's share in the global bamboo market is almost negligible.

Figure 3: Countries with the Largest Bamboo Resources

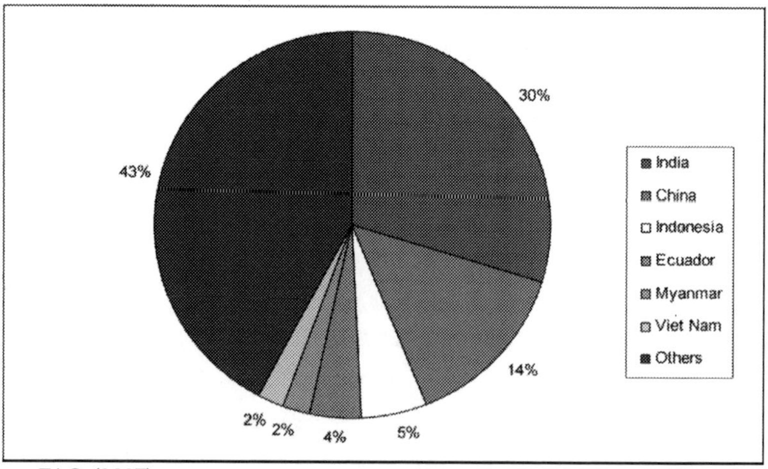

Source: FAO (2007).

Figure 4: Status of Hydropower Potential Development in India

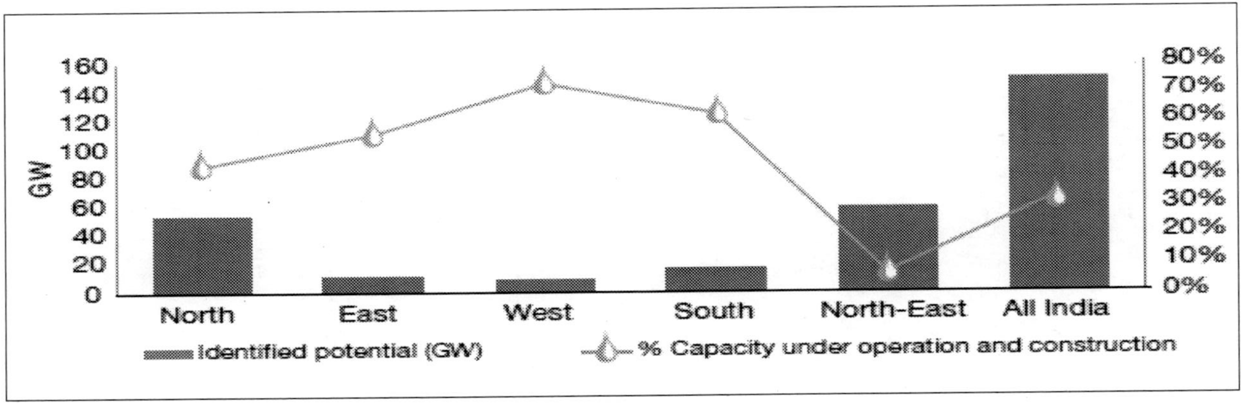

Source: https://www.pwc.in/assets/pdfs/publications/2014/hydropower-in-india-key-enablers-for-better-tomorrow.pdf

Table 2 below shows that China, which has just 14 percent share in the global production, enjoys more than 65 percent share in the global bamboo export market. India, on the other hand, has less than 1 percent share. Surprisingly, despite having enormous bamboo reserves, India is the third largest importer of bamboo products in the world with a share of 1.51 percent of the global import. In the year 2012, China exported nearly 1238 USD million worth bamboo and rattan products like bamboo shoots (241 USD million), bamboo woven products (375 USD million), industrialised bamboo products (413 USD million), furniture (54 USD million). Its leading trade partners were USA (25 percent), EU (20 percent), Japan (20 percent), Australia (4 percent) and Malaysia (3 percent).

Table 2: Highlight of Global Bamboo Trade in 2012

Country	Export share	Country	Import share
China	65.81	Canada	2.85
Indonesia	9.34	China	1.70
Viet Nam	4.55	India	1.51
Philippines	1.91	Malaysia	0.54
India	0.11	Viet Nam	0.21
Others	18.27	Others	93.19

Source: INBAR 2012.

Likewise China, NER can also become a major bamboo exporter in the world with the help of proper strategies and practices. Small scale bamboo processing units could be established in the region using PPP framework and products like boiled bamboo shoots, furniture, handicrafts, etc., can be exported to neighbouring ASEAN and its member countries like Thailand, Japan, Malaysia, etc.

Hydropower

Being the third fastest growing region in the world, the demand for power in Southeast Asia is projected to grow at an increasing rate over the next few decades. By 2040, ASEAN needs to produce

354 GW more power (more than double of its existing capacity) to sustain the economic progress (IEA 2015). Though ASEAN countries are rich in energy resources, meeting this high demand will be challenging. One such opportunity lies in India's NER which is rich in hydropower resources. With 148 GW, India ranks fifth in the world in terms of usable hydropower potential and NER has nearly 42.54 percent share in country's total potential. However, nearly 93 percent hydropower potential in NER is yet to be harnessed. This sharply contrasts the scenarios in south and western region where more than 65 percent of the total potential has already been harnessed. Central Electric Authority (CEA) has identified 168 large dams in the Brahmaputra basin. By exploiting the potential hydropower opportunities, NER can not only satisfy the domestic demand but also supply to the ASEAN and other East Asian countries. However, this requires investment, technical know-how, consensus building with the locals, obtaining necessary approvals from the statutory bodies, etc. By leveraging the AEP, NER can integrate itself with the ASEAN regional power system and help meeting the rising power demand in the region.

Conclusion

Act East Policy is pregnant with all the potentials to escort NER out of underdevelopment and poverty. It is important that we recognise the centrality of NER in AEP. For this purpose, statutory provisions are required to empower these bordering states in the region to enter into cross-border business deals. However, centrality of NER itself will not guarantee the development of NER, unless the foot-soldiers of development of the region (politicians, bureaucrats, entrepreneurs, academicians, activists) do not deliver at the ground, the fruits of AEP will also remain elusive in NER.

REFERENCES

Community Forest International (CFI) (2006) Forest sector review of northeast India. Accessed on https://goo.gl/kIKzgH on July 28, 2016.

Das G., Das SC and Paul UK, 'Look East Policy: economic engagements with ASEAN and East Asian countries', in *Look East to Act East Policy: Implications for India's Northeast*, G Das and CJ Thomas (eds.), New York: Routledge, 2016.

Food and Agricultural Organisation (FAO) (2007) World bamboo resources: A thematic study prepared in the framework of the Global Forest Resources Assessment 2005. Accessed on http://www.fao.org/3/a-a1243e.pdf on June 22, 2016.

International Trade of Bamboo and Rattan (INBR) (2012) International trade of bamboo and rattan. Accessed from https://goo.gl/XAMb0z on August 2, 2016.

6

Five Decades of ASEAN:

An Indian Perspective

V. Suryanarayan

The year 2017 will be an important milestone in the evolution of Association of Southeast Asian Nations (ASEAN) as a regional organisation. During these five decades, Southeast Asia in general, and ASEAN in particular, had to face innumerable inter-related domestic and international challenges. In this paper, I propose to provide an Indian perspective on the challenges facing ASEAN today and whether it will continue to function as a united and vibrant regional organisation.

Many commentators have projected ASEAN as a dynamic economic organisation; however, it must be pointed out that its success was mainly in the field of political co-operation. The formation of ASEAN itself was a political act, though political co-operation was not specifically mentioned in the ASEAN declaration. On the 20th anniversary of ASEAN, former Malaysian Prime Minister Dr. Mahathir pointed out: 'In its first twenty years, the main thrust of ASEAN has been political. This is, as it should be, and we have no need for regrets.'[1] Dr Mahathir added, 'None of the ASEAN countries would have developed economically if the political wrangling could not be solved.'[2]

Ghazalie Shafie, former Malaysian Foreign Minister, during the Third Indo-China War, when many commentators projected ASEAN as a model for regional co-operation, 'likened ASEAN to a cluster of bamboos, each of which was an independent entity, and which together could withstand turbulent winds; the tallest of the bamboos must always stoop its head. Indonesia is a large country, but it has never imposed its will on other ASEAN countries'.[3] Adam Malik, Indonesian Foreign Minister, who first proposed the formation of a regional organisation in Southeast Asia, echoed the same feelings. To quote: "Although from the outset ASEAN was conceived as an organisation for economic, social and cultural co-operation...it was the fact that there was convergence of political outlook...which provided the main stimulus to join together in ASEAN".[4]

It must, however, be pointed out that throughout the formative years, Southeast Asian countries could neither influence regional developments nor bring about any major change in the attitude of super powers. The author would like to illustrate one incident which cast a long shadow on Singapore-Indonesia relations. During the Konfrontasi, in 1964, two Indonesian guerrillas blasted a bomb in the Singapore branch of Hong Kong and Shanghai Bank in Orchard Road. The bomb blast resulted in the death of three Singapore citizens. The Indonesian guerrillas were tried according to Singapore law and were awarded capital punishment in October 1968. The political climate, by then, had undergone a radical transformation in Southeast Asia. Sukarno had fallen, Suharto had come to power and Konfrontasi had come to an end. What is more, both President Suharto and Prime Minister Tunku Abdul Rahman appealed to Lee Kuan Yew to show clemency and not to hang the guerrillas. Lee Kuan Yew adopted a holier than thou attitude and hanged the guerrillas. His objective was to prove to his people and the international community that three million Singaporeans could stand up against 130 million Indonesians. When the dead bodies reached Indonesia, there were large scale anti-Chinese riots. The Singapore Embassy in Jakarta was ransacked. The riots spread from Jakarta to Central Java and Sumatra. A long spell of chilled relations between the two countries followed. And when finally Lee Kuan Yew made an official visit to Indonesia in May 1973 he had to place a wreath in the Kalibata Heroes Cemetery where the Indonesian guerrillas were buried.

The chill in Singapore-Indonesia relations was not an isolated incident. Mention should be made of Filipino claim to Sabah; Thai suspicions that separatist feelings in Southern Thailand were being encouraged by Malay politicians in Malaysia; the visit of Israeli President Cham Herzog to Singapore which resulted in anti-Israeli and anti-Singapore demonstrations; Singapore's negativestance on the Indonesian annexation of the Portuguese Colony of East Timor; Singapore's opposition to the Malaysian initiative to speed up the process of self-determination in Brunei—all these triggered storms. But it goes to the credit of leaders of ASEAN that they did not allow these incidents to go completely out of control. South Asia can learn a lot from the political behaviour of ASEAN leaders.

Indian and Chinese Response to the Formation of ASEAN

The formation of ASEAN synchronised with the intensification of the Vietnam War. What is more, member states of ASEAN were in varying degrees aligned to the United States. China attacked ASEAN as a military alliance set up by the "reactionaries of five countries at the behest of US imperialism". It maintained that behind the façade of economic co-operation was the reality of ASEAN—"a military alliance specifically directed against China". New Delhi was also not enthusiastic about the formation of ASEAN because it would further plunge Southeast Asia into the cockpit of super power rivalry. Even then, New Delhi's reservations about ASEAN never reached the level of strident

Chinese criticism that Lee Kuan Yew, Tunku Abdul Rahman and Suharto were the running dogs of the imperialists.[5]

The Cultural Revolution further widened the schism between China and ASEAN. China's strident revolutionary line and call for People War led to the resurgence of communist parties. During this period through underground radio stations located in Southern China the Chinese Communist Party extended powerful ideological support to pro-Peking Communist parties in the region. The net result was the strengthening image of the image of China as a destablising force.[6]

US-China: Establishment of Diplomatic Relations

The secret visit by Henry Kissinger to China in July 1971 and subsequent establishment of diplomatic relations transformed international relations. Mao Tse Tung wanted to end his country's diplomatic isolation by following an ancient Chinese stratagem; pitting the barbarians against each other; enlist the support of the far away enemy (United States) against the more dangerous enemy next door (Soviet Union). President Nixon invoked Wilsonian principles to invite China to join the comity of nations. In an article in the Foreign Affairs, Nixon wrote: 'We simply cannot afford to leave China forever outside the family of nations, there to nurture its fantasies, cherish its hates and threaten its neighbours. There is no place on this small planet for a billion of its potentially most able people to live in angry isolation'.[7]

Kissinger's visit to Beijing culminating in the establishment of diplomatic relations with China came as a bolt from the blue to US allies in South East Asia. They were completely taken unawares. They had no other option but to follow the US lead. Each country did it in its own way. The Malaysian Government began to champion the establishment of a Zone of Peace, Freedom and Neutrality (ZOPHAN) in Southeast Asia, to be guaranteed by the great powers, especially by China. The other members of ASEAN had their reservations but the Malaysian diplomats were able to persuade ASEAN in 1971 to accept ZOPHAN as its long-term goal. Malaysia was the first country to establish diplomatic relations with China in May 1974; it was followed by the Philippines in June 1975; Thailand in July 1975; Indonesia re-established diplomatic relations in December 1989 and Singapore in October 1980. Lee Kuan Yew did not want to give the impression that Chinese-dominated Singapore was in a hurry to establish diplomatic relations with China. He had made it clear that it will be the last among ASEAN to establish diplomatic relations with China; however, there were regular exchanges between the two countries, what is more, bilateral trade had taken a quantum jump.

ASEAN Unity at its Best – Third Indo-China War

The Vietnamese invasion of Cambodia by Vietnam in December 1978 spurred ASEAN to forge unity and rally behind Thailand, the frontline state. With the support of United States and China, ASEAN was able to isolate Vietnam in the comity of nations. In that process, ASEAN provided legitimacy to the genocidal regime of Pol Pot-Ieng Sary clique as the ruling group in Cambodia. Later ASEAN was able to persuade China to back a united front led by Sihanouk; but, Sihanouk was only a titular head, and behind him was the ugly face of Pol Pot and Ieng Sary. It must be pointed out that behind the façade of unity, each member state of ASEAN had its own assessment of the long-term objectives of China in Southeast Asia. Indonesia, and to a certain extent, Malaysia subscribed to the view that the reason behind Vietnamese invasion of Cambodia and installation of Heng Samrin government in power was due to its fear that Pol Pot, backed by China, was a threat to Vietnam's security. They were keen to create a situation, where Hanoi could become an independent centre of power and remain as a bulwark against Chinese expansionism in Southeast Asia.[8] It is interesting to note that Benny Murdani, the Indonesian Army Chief, after a visit to Vietnam declared that Vietnam had no expansionist designs in Southeast Asia. However, neither Malaysia nor Indonesia wanted to act as an obstacle to unity and, therefore, went along with other member states to safeguard Thailand's interests. Lee Kuan Yew was the most hawkish among the ASEAN leaders in defence of China's policy towards Vietnam. An illustration is the speech he delivered in the meeting of the CHOGM in New Delhi in 1980. Lee Kuan Yew cited two major events that adversely affected international relations, namely Vietnamese invasion of Cambodia and second, Soviet intervention in Afghanistan. In the considered view of "non-aligned" Singapore China's invasion of Vietnam did not take place at all.[9] No wonder, India's relations with Southeast Asia, during this period, reached an all time low.

China's Policy of Winning Friends and Influencing People in Southeast Asia

With the ascendancy of Deng Xiao Ping in power in China, the policy of liberalisation commenced in a big way. Deng began to articulate a vision of China, which will play an important role commensurate to its size, economic resources and historical traditions. As Henry Kissinger has pointed out Deng was convinced that modern technology will have to be introduced in China, thousands of Chinese students should be sent abroad for higher studies and, what is more, past mistakes have to be avoided.[10] As a result, foreign direct investment was encouraged, export promotion zones were established and building of infrastructure was given top priority. China today has become the factory of the world. Henry Kissinger has rightly concluded: 'The China of today—with the world's second largest economy and largest volume of foreign exchange reserves, and with multiple cities boasting skyscrapers taller than the Emperor State Building—is a testimony to Deng's vision, tenacity, and common sense'.[11]

The modernisation of China can take place only in a peaceful environment and, therefore, Beijing relegated the contentious issues to the background. What brought Beijing and Southeast Asian countries closer was China's astute economic diplomacy. When Southeast Asian countries were engulfed in a serious economic crisis in the late 1980s and international financial institutions and developing countries like Japan and Singapore were not forthcoming in extending assistance, China played its cards cleverly. There was general fear that China may devalue its currency to boost up its exports to Southeast Asian countries. Not only China resisted this temptation, what is more, it entered into long-term trade agreements with Southeast Asian countries to stabilise their economies. China has emerged as the major trading partner of all Southeast Asian countries. The end result is interdependence in the economic sphere whether it is with United States, European Union or Southeast Asia. As a result, pro-China lobbies have become powerful in all these countries.

Transformation in China–Southeast Asia relations can be illustrated with special reference to Malaysia and Singapore. When China attacked India in 1962, Tunku Abdul Rahman, Prime Minister of the Federation of Malaya, was on a state visit to India. Federation of Malaya was the first country to extend its wholehearted support to India. After his return to Kuala Lumpur the Tunku started a 'save democracy fund' to assist India in its defence preparedness. But Malaysian perception of China has undergone a transformation and today Kuala Lumpur perceives China as a benign force in Southeast Asia. In his Memoirs, A Doctor in the House: Memoirs of Tun Mahahir Mohammad, the former Malaysian Prime Minister, has written: 'I stuck up good relations with the Chinese leaders, in particular with Ziang Zemin. Malaysia's goodwill and support are well known to most informed Chinese citizens. China has become the world's factory, churning out all kinds of manufactured goods which are very quickly achieving world standards. Their per capita income is below that of Malaysia, but their population makes China a huge market. Malaysia is China's largest trading partner in Southeast Asia and our trade volume continues to grow. I hope our China friendly foreign policy will continue. We must not fall into the American trap of regarding China as a potential enemy. When you regard a country as a potential enemy, you can be sure that country will regard you as its current enemy'.[12]

Over the years, Singapore's view of China has undergone great changes. Two examples are given below to prove this point. S.R. Nathan, former President of Singapore, describes an incident during Lee Kuan Yew's visit to China in 1976. The highlight of the visit was Lee Kuan Yew's meeting with the Chinese Foreign Minister Hua Guofeng. During the discussion Hua presented the Prime Minister with a book saying, 'This is the correct account of the war between India and China. I hope you will find it useful'. Lee Kuan Yew looked at the book, looked at the front cover, looked at the back, and said, 'Mr. Prime Minister, this is your version of the war. There is another version, Indian version. And, in any case, I am from Southeast Asia. It has nothing to do with us'. He handed the book back. For me this was a very important moment, a clear confirmation that Lee Kuan Yew, although ethnically Chinese, was his own man, in no way subordinate to China or the Chinese communists. We in Singapore had a separate multi-racial identity. What we made clear is that we should not be taken for granted. The Chinese Foreign Minister Qiao Guanhua was rather agitated, but kept his cool; his wife did not; and walked out of the room in a huff'[13] Nearly four decades later another incident took place which brings out in sharp focus the change in Singapore's perception of China. George Yeo, the former Singapore Foreign Minister, went to China in September 2011. The Chinese authorities arranged a meeting between their nominee of Panchan Lama and George Yeo. It may be stated that George Yeo visited Tibet during his earlier visit and was in full praise of China's efforts to bring about massive economic transformation. What does this event signal? Does it mean that in the post-Dalai Lama phase Singapore will support China's nominee as the leader of the Tibetan people?

Late B. Raman, India's leading strategic specialist, posed the question as follows: 'The action of the Singapore Foreign Minister in providing legitimacy to the actions of the Chinese Communist Party in interfering with the religious affairs of the Tibetan Buddhists and tampering with their traditions cannot be missed'.[14]

In the economic transformation of China, Singapore statesman Lee Kuan Yew has played a very significant role. Lee Kuan Yew and Deng Xiao Ping were both Hakkas, which created a strong bond between the two leaders. Lee Kuan Yew explained the contrast between the Overseas Chinese and those who remained in China. The Overseas Chinese are the descendants of those poor people who migrated from the famine-stricken areas of South China. But by sheer hard work and perseverance they today control the economies of all Southeast Asian countries. Lee pointed out to Deng that the Chinese can do better than Singapore. To quote Lee: 'I countered that they should have no problem in getting ahead and doing much better than Singapore, because we are the descendants of the illiterate, landless peasants from Fujian and Guangdong, while they had the progeny of the scholars, Mandarins and literati who had stayed at home. He was silent'.[15] Obviously Deng was impressed with the achievements of Singapore and was trying to find out ways and means as to how to involve Singapore in the economic transformation of China. More than Lee Kuan Yew, it was Goh Keng Swee who advised China how to start the export promotion zones and industrial parks. Equally relevant the Overseas Chinese business men were persuaded to invest in China in a big way. While it is very difficult to calculate the exact investment made by the Overseas Chinese, many commentators have pointed that nearly 70 per cent of the FDI has come from the Overseas Chinese in Hong Kong, Taiwan and Southeast Asian countries.[16]

China follows an Assertive Foreign Policy

Keen students of China's foreign policy can notice an important change in China's foreign policy during recent years. China no longer supports revolutionary struggles as it did during the first and second Indo-Chinese wars. On the contrary, it has started behaving like the United States. In order to promote its national interests, Beijing has propped up reactionary and anti-democratic governments in South and Southeast Asian countries. China's under-writing the Pol Pot-Ieng Sary clique in Cambodia, its propping up the military regime in Myanmar, its close alliance with successive Pakistani governments in their nuclear programmes, China's support to the genocidal Mahinda Rajapaksa government in Sri Lanka during the Fourth Eelam War – are clear illustrations that Beijing will go to any extreme in furtherance of its national interests. With Deng Xiao Ping out of the scene his successors are asserting China's territorial claims in its neighbourhood. What is more, this assertive policy is taking place at a time, when ASEAN has become a house divided.

South China Sea – Likely Flash Point in Southeast Asia

The outcome of the Second Indo-China War, in retrospect, was not only a humiliating defeat for the United States, it was, in equal measure, a debacle for China. As Kissinger has mentioned: "A united communist-led Vietnam, victorious in its second war in 1975, would turn out to be a far greater strategic threat to China than to the United States.[17] The proud and self-confident Vietnam began to pursue an independent foreign policy, but in the light of China's strident opposition, Hanoi had no other option but to join COMECON and later enter into a defence treaty with the Soviet Union.

Even before the Second Indo-China War ended Vietnamese Navy took over the Spratly group of islands which were under the control of the South Vietnamese Navy. Hanoi was eager that China should not meddle in South China Sea and published a colour map of Vietnam showing not only the Spratlys, but also the China-occupied Paracel islands as Vietnamese territory.

South China Sea occupies an area of 3.5 million square kilometres, about the size of India. There are conflicting territorial claims; the claimants are China, Taiwan, Vietnam, the Philippines, Brunei, Malaysia and Indonesia. If China's claims were to be conceded, 90 per cent of South China Sea would come under Beijing's control. It is made up of 150 specks of land, coral reef and sand banks. The fishing grounds are frequented by Chinese, Vietnamese and Filipino fishermen. More important the vast oil resources are coveted by all littoral states. China and Vietnam has embarked upon oil exploration in a big way. China has taken an unambiguous stand that the border dispute should be resolved through bilateral dialogue and, on several occasions, has expressed its readiness to do so. ASEAN, on the other hand, is of the view that the dispute should be resolved multilaterally through dialogue and consultation.

The unanimous verdict given by the Tribunal (delivered on July 12, 2016) constituted under Article VII of the UNCLOS in the case filed by the Philippines against China has naturally resulted in a major controversy. The verdict is a major setback for China. It must, however, be pointed out that China did not participate in the proceedings of the Tribunal and repeatedly affirmed that the Tribunal has no jurisdiction to arbitrate on the issue. The major findings of the verdict can be summarised as follows: 1) The five member commission gave the unanimous decision in favour of the Philippines. There is no evidence to prove that China had historically exercised exclusive control over the waters or their resources. The rights claimed by China within the "nine-dash line" are illegal. 2) The Tribunal noted that the reefs have been modified by land reclamation and inflicted irreparable damage to marine environment. China has violated the sovereign rights of the Philippines in its exclusive economic zone. 3) China has interfered with fishing and oil exploratory rights of Philippines. It has thus created a serious risk of collision at sea. 4) The Tribunal concluded that there was no legal basis for China to claim historical rights to resources in the South China Sea and 5) The Tribunal, however, added that the root of the dispute lies in "fundamentally different understandings of their respective rights" under UNCLOS in the waters of the South China Sea.[18]

The question naturally arises: What is the United States policy towards judgments given by the International Court of Justice (ICJ)? The United States had an uneasy relationship with the ICJ, which primarily arbitrates on cases between members of the United Nations that recognize its jurisdiction. The United States withdrew from the Court's compulsory jurisdiction in 1986 after the Court ruled that it owed Nicaragua war reparations. The United States also disagreed with the Court's stance that it failed to fulfil its obligations under the Vienna Convention on consular relations in 2005 in cases involving Mexican nationals on death row.[19] China naturally will cite these cases; how will the United States justify itself and, at the same time, uphold the Hague Judgment in the South China Sea case.

ASEAN Response

The unanimous verdict of the international Tribunal must have been a matter of great jubilation for the Filipino government. On the contrary the newly elected President Rodrigo Duterte has declared that he is willing to enter into negotiations with China for joint development of South China Sea. This statement marks a distinct departure from the policies of the previous government, which had been extremely critical of China's assertive claims in the South China Sea. The previous Government had also filed a case in the International Court of Justice. Will the new President succumb to the 'cheque book diplomacy' of the Chinese Government? Will the path of negotiations lead to domestic tensions within the country? How will the United States respond to the new initiatives of President Rodrigo Duterte?

It must be pointed out that China's policy towards Southeast Asia has paid rich dividends. ASEAN is no longer a homogenous unit. In the earlier summits, attempts made by Vietnam and the Philippines to persuade other members to adopt a critical approach towards China on the territorial claims in South China sea did not succeed. Finally the summit concluded with passing a resolution appealing to all parties concerned that they should strive for an amicable solution.

Member states of ASEAN hope that the United States would continue to maintain its military presence in Southeast Asia, whereas China is convinced that Washington will disengage from Southeast Asia sooner or later. Time, therefore, is on China's side. Singapore statesman Lee Kuan Yew was of the view that the United States and China need not confront in Southeast Asia. There is sufficient space for both countries to co-exist in the region. In a conversation with American scholars Graham Allison and Robert D Blackwill, published in a book entitled Grand Master's Insights into China, Lee Kuan Yew said: 'Competition between United States and China is inevitable, but conflict is not. This is not Cold War. The Soviet Union was contesting with the United States for global supremacy. China is acting purely in national interest. It is not interested in changing the world. China needs the United States, needs US markets, needs technology, and needs to have students going to the United States. There is no irreconcilable ideological conflict between United States and China that has enthusiastically embraced the market'.[20]

China and Settlement of Border Disputes

China is the only country which has used force to buttress its territorial claims—against India in 1962, against Soviet Union in 1969, against Vietnam in 1979 and against the Philippines in 1995. In addition to bilateral tensions, there was also an international dimension on conflicts with India and Vietnam—the Cuban missile crisis in 1962 and China-US strategic entente in 1979. China's punitive expedition against Vietnam took place only after Deng Xiao Ping's visit to the United States and detailed discussions with

Brzezinski. As Henry Kissinger has rightly pointed out: 'The Third Vietnam War was the high point of Sino-American strategic co-operation during the Cold War'.[21] We have to keep in mind this reality while analysing China's policy towards border claims in the South China Sea.

Middle Kingdom Mentality

Perceptive students of Chinese history are conscious of the reality that China, whenever it becomes strong and united, displays the Middle Kingdom mentality. The Chinese called their country the 'Middle Kingdom' or the centre of the Universe. All other countries in the neighbourhood were its vassals. In other words what is happening in South China Sea is an attempt to impose Chinese hegemony. Equally relevant, the Chinese leaders are experts in putting into practice the teachings of the Chinese strategic thinker Sun Tzu. According to Sun Tzu, China should win victories where battles will be unnecessary. China's astute diplomacy that has resulted in divisions within ASEAN is an illustration of the validity of Sun Tzu in contemporary China. And if force is to be used, China will not have any hesitation to employ it.

Conclusion

In his monumental book, *The Study of History*, Prof. Arnold Toynbee analyses the rise and fall of civilisations. He traces how civilisations originate, how they develop, how they decay and how they get destroyed. Most of the civilisations which developed in different parts of the world have disappeared, but only two civilisations have shown remarkable continuity that is the Indic and Sinic civilisations. According to Prof. Toynbee, these two civilisations will inevitably clash in the geographical region between them and the Sinic civilisation will ultimately triumph. To quote Toynbee's prophetic words: 'In the end, the current of Chinese expansion will meet the current of Hindu expansion over the submerged heads of the smaller and weaker and less efficient peoples in between who are going asunder. And after that has happened, I surmise that the new frontier between India and China will tend, slowly but surely, to travel westward at India's expense and in China's favour'.[22]

Will the words of Prof. Toynbee, almost prophetic, come true? Will China emerge as the sole hegemonic power in Southeast Asia? Or will the Southeast Asian leaders display resilience so that they can retain their political and cultural identities? And, what is more, will New Delhi pursue a more dynamic Act East Policy, which will contribute to independence, stability and prosperity of Southeast Asian peoples? Time alone can provide an answer.

**This essay is partly based on Author's earlier writings on the subject.*

REFERENCES

1. Mahathir Mohammad, 'Keynote address at the first ASEAN Economic Conference', in *ASEAN at the Crossroads: Obstacles, Options and Opportunities in Economic Co-operation*, Noordin Soipee (ed.), Kuala Lumpur, 1987, p.1.
2. Ibid.
3. Tan Sri Ghazalie Shafie, 'Experience of ASEAN and Prospects of ASEAN-SAARC Co-operation', in *Shaping South Asia's Future: Role of Regional Co-operation*, Kant Kishore Bhargava, Heinz Bongartz and Farooz Sobhan (eds.), New Delhi, 1995, pp.97–103.
4. Roger Irvine, 'The Formative Years of ASEAN, 1967-1975',, in *Understanding ASEAN*, Alison Broinowski (ed.), London, 1982, p.14.
5. For details refer, V. Suryanarayan, Malaysia's China Policy: 1957-1974 (Monograph 4, Centre for South and Southeast Asian Studies, University of Madras, 1980).
6. Ibid.
7. Henry Kissinger, *On China*, London, p. 203, 2011.
8. V. Suryanarayan, 'The Challenge of Kampuchea', in *Yearbook on India's Foreign Policy, 1989*, Satish Kumar (ed.), New Delhi, 1990, pp.97–104.
9. V. Suryanarayan, 'An Indian Perspective on ASEAN, Hanoi and the Security of Southeast Asia', *Indian Yearbook of International Affairs*, University of Madras, Madras, Vol. XIX, pp. 595–608.
10. Kissinger, n.7, op. cit., p. 321.
11. Ibid., pp. 330–-31
12. Mahathir Mohammad, *Doctor in the House: Memoirs of Tun Mohammad Mahathir Mohammad*, Kuala Lumpur, 2011, p. 432.
13. S.R. Nathan, *An Unexpected Journey: Path to Presidency*, Singapore, 2011, p. 424.

14. V. Suryanarayan, 'China and Southeast Asia', in *Rise of China: Implications for India*, D.S. Rajan, R.S. Vasan and J.A. Bonofer (eds). (Chennai, 2012), pp. 29–48
15. Lee Kuan Yew, *From Third World to First, The Singapore Story, 1965- 2000 (Memoirs of Lee Kuan Yew)*, Singapore, 2000, p. 662
16. V. Suryanarayan, 'People's Republic of China's Policy towards Overseas Chinese', *Indian Perspectives on China*, D.S. Rajan (ed.), Vol. 2, New Delhi, 2013, pp. 137–54.
17. Kissinger, n.7, op. cit., p. 343.
18. Press Release. The South China Sea Arbitration (The Republic of the Philippines v. The Republic of China) The Hague, 12 July 2016.
19. Council on Foreign Relations, The United States and the ICJ, September 27, 2011.
20. V. Suryanarayan, 'China's Transformation: Role of Lee Kuan Yew', in *China in Transition: Implications for Asia*, G Thangarajesh and P. Vithiapathy (eds.), Chennai, 2015, pp. 52–60.
21. Kissinger, n. 7, op. cit., p. 341.

7

India-ASEAN Economic Integration:

Need to Address Political and Security Concerns

H. Srikanth

The Fourth Roundtable on ASEAN-India Network of Think Tanks (AINTT) organised in the capital city of Kuala Lumpur in Malaysia on 7-8th of August 2015, devoted quite a few sessions to discuss the common security concerns and the civilisational ties that India and ASEAN countries have. Some representatives from Business and Industry raised objections to the Round Table's emphasis on security and cultural concerns and expressed the view that valuable time was wasted debating over non-economic issues ignoring the economic issues which forms the core of India-ASEAN engagement. They insisted that focus of the Round Table should be on trade, business and industry. True, economic issues are vital and there is a need for in-depth discussion on problems, policies and prospects of economic relations between India and ASEAN. But does that preclude us from appreciating the significance of political and security concerns that facilitate or retard the economic relations between the countries in the region? Pointing out the key political and security concerns, this paper emphasises on humane handling of the non-economic contradictions within and between the countries that is vital for promoting the relations between India and ASEAN.

There is no doubt that India's engagement with ASEAN is motivated primarily by economic concerns. Political and economic developments like the collapse of the Soviet Union, the foreign exchange crisis, the resurgence of market forces, etc., have compelled India's Look East Policy and India's desire to revive its relations with Southeast Asian countries. As the secure market that India had with the Soviet Bloc disappeared, it became necessary for India to look towards the East for promoting its trade and investment opportunities. Similarly, the end of the Cold War, the rise of China and the US's initial preoccupation with West Asia, compelled ASEAN to befriend India. India took proactive interest in strengthening its relations with ASEAN and starting as a dialogue partner, now it has become a full member of ASEAN Regional Forum (ARF) and East Asia Summit. There is no doubt that India's support to different sub-regional connectivity projects, India's financial assistance to Myanmar and other weaker ASEAN countries, and India's willingness to negotiate free trade agreements with ASEAN countries are motivated by economic interests. However, economic objectives cannot be fulfilled merely by constructing roads, improving communication and transport and concluding Free Trade Agreements. Economic agenda remains unfulfilled if one ignores political and security concerns which set the environment for economic engagement between nations.

History shows that mature political leadership that thinks beyond immediate domestic compulsions and petty party politics is vital to the success of country's foreign policy. It is a known fact that one of the compulsions for India going in for engagement with and Southeast Asia is our failure to build South Asian Association for Regional Cooperation (SAARC) as an effective and cohesive regional body. SAARC was also formed with the noble idea of addressing the common problems of the South Asian countries by encouraging understanding and cooperation among the member nations. Had the SAARC experiment succeeded, it would have contributed to better economic integration and ensured India's economic interests as well. Despite its centrality in South Asia, India failed to lead SAARC, partly because of the smaller nations' fear of India's domination, and partly because of India's failure to build confidence among the neighbouring countries. Differences and animosities between India and Pakistan did not allow SAARC to emerge as an effective regional organisation. Taking lessons from the failure of its diplomacy in SAARC, India should be extra cautious in the way it handles our East and Southeast Asian neighbours. India doesn't need to confront Pakistan on the eastern front, but China continues to be a factor in India-ASEAN relations. Although there is not much of bad blood between India and ASEAN countries, socio-economic differences between the countries can mar the prospects of healthy economic relations between the nations, if the member nations fail to deal with them in a matured way. On its part, India should avoid being unduly scared of its adversary, China, and at the same time, resist the temptation to dominate weak ASEAN countries like Myanmar. Big or small, every nation has its own identity and glorious history. No nation likes to be bullied and looked down up on by bigger and more powerful nations. It is necessary to respect every nation's concern for national sovereignty, unity and integrity, and avoid meddling in internal politics of other nations. While helping the small and poorer nations, India in its own interest should avoid playing the role of a Big Brother. India should realise that it cannot be a bully like the US or even Israel. Indulging in adventurism, such as undertaking surgical strikes in Myanmar without the consent of the Government of Myanmar, is counter-productive. Surgical strikes may make sense against an enemy country, not against countries like Myanmar, whose cooperation is indispensable for the success of the government's Look/Act East Policy. Irrespective of which party or alliance of parties is in power, the time-tested Principles of *Panchsheel*, which emphasise on cooperation based on mutual respect and trust and non-interference in the internal affairs of the countries, should remain guidance for India's engagement with other nations.

Further, economic relations between the neighbouring countries can grow if only the countries feel secure. Threats to national security come from without and from within. Secure borders are essential conditions for good relations between the neighbours. India has dispute with Pakistan over the issue of Kashmir, that cannot be resolved in the near future. The border situation on the eastern side which was also grim for decades appears to be getting better. Although border dispute between China and India are not yet resolved, both countries started reviving working relations with each other. Cessation of hostilities across the borders definitely paved the way for promoting economic relations between India and China. Amicable settlement of border disputes provides a sense of security and promotes economic cooperation between the countries. Recently India and Bangladesh have also taken positive steps to end border disputes by ratifying the agreement over the swapping of the enclaves. Such positive steps indeed help both the countries to improve economic relations between the two countries. Settlement of border disputes, respecting the sovereign rights of the states over their territories, not allowing one's territory to be used for anti-national activities of other countries, and cooperating with the neighbouring countries in fighting the terrorism and transnational crimes are essential conditions for good economic relations between nations.

Security problems are not always the result of external enemies. The border areas of many a nation state in South Asia and Southeast Asia are sites of ethnic insurgencies and secessionist movements. India has been witnessing ethnic insurgencies in the border states of Assam, Arunachal Pradesh, Nagaland and Manipur. Many such movements are visible in all peripheral regions of Myanmar. Many of the transnational connectivity projects that India, China and ASEAN have conceived would pass through the territories controlled by militant groups fighting for autonomy or independence. These groups, which often indulge in terrorist and criminal activities, have the power to blockade the roads, impose illegal taxes and disrupt the movement of the vehicles and the people. Underdevelopment, unemployment and sense of alienation that the people experience breed growth of ethnic militancy in the peripheral regions. These protests cannot be put down only by military. Appropriate interventions are needed to put an end to insurgencies and secessionist movements. Without neutralising the militant organisations and securing the lives of the people in the border states, it is not possible to establish peace and order essential for effective operation of the proposed connectivity projects.

Finally, we all need to learn lessons from experience of the European Union. Till the other day European Union (EU) was a model for economic integration of nations. But the crisis in Greece and the exit of UK from the European Union indicate that the EU Model has its own constraints. When countries at different stages of development with different political systems, history and cultural backgrounds come together, there are bound to be contradictions. Economic cooperation is possible only when all the member nations and all communities and classes of people living within the nations feel that they are all equal partners and that integration of the national economies are in their interest. Lack of trust and fear of domination hamper the prospects of mutually beneficial economic relations. Development projects will not receive popular support, if they benefit only the elites. The governments' efforts to liberalise and globalise the national economies will meet with popular resistance, if they are meant only to protect and promote the interests of the corporate sector. It is therefore essential for the governments to ensure that development projects they initiate are inclusive, participatory and democratic in spirit and in action. Consent, support and active participation of the people living in the border areas are essential for the success of the projects aimed at integration of the national economies.

Adequate attention should therefore be given to the economic and non-economic concerns of the citizens, especially of those living along the national borders. ASEAN leaders did in fact understand the need to address the problems of poverty, unemployment, health and insecurity, and incorporated it in the Bali Concord Declaration, 2003. If ASEAN–Indian relations are to improve, India also should not ignore the problems, fears, concerns and expectations of the people living on either side of the borders. For decades, the national security concerns led India to view its border people with suspicion and neglected the economic development of the region. The border states were militarised and every kind of protest in the region is viewed from mainstream national perspectives. The people's sense of alienation, their legitimate aspirations for autonomy and demands for redressal of their grievances are not adequately and efficiently addressed. This neglect has led to the birth of different kinds of protest movements. Rightly or wrongly the people in the north-eastern region look at every move of the central government with suspicion. Since many of the India's ASEAN projects pass through north-eastern states, it is essential that the governments address the genuine concerns of the peoples of the northeast and win over their support for its Look or Act East policy. Integration of national economies and militarisation of borders cannot go together. What is said of India is true of its ASEAN neighbours as well. The success of ASEAN-India projects of economic integration and development depends to a considerable extent on how effectively political leadership in India and ASEAN handle both internal and external contradictions in a mature way and clear all the obstacles standing in the way of economic cooperation and development of all countries in the region.

8

Why Engaging Myanmar is Important?

Munmun Majumdar

India's policy of looking east[1] is not new. However, the contexts and thrusts of India's approach to the region have changed. Given India's economic reforms from early 1990s and the attendant effort to integrate with regional and global economy, India's Look-East Policy had undoubtedly assumed a greater economic dimension, particularly in its relations with the ASEAN[2] countries. Another very important dimension was that the policy was also linked with India's domestic considerations as it was a ground-breaking attempt to link India's landlocked Northeastern states with the economies of the ASEAN region. The Narendra Modi-led government that came into power in 2014 accorded high priority to India's Look-East Policy. During his opening statement at the 12th ASEAN summit, he underscored the importance of the 10-nation ASEAN bloc in a new era of economic development, trade, investments and industrialisation. He made known to the world that India is not merely 'Looking East' but is now 'Acting East' as well, thus, revising the title to 'India's Act-East Policy'.[3] The government in 2015 upgraded the Look-East Policy to Act-East Policy,[4] which continues to be driven by economic and security interests and is extended beyond Southeast Asia underlining the importance of the geopolitics of the region.

In this the role of Myanmar is crucial[5] because India cannot afford to ignore the geopolitical reality of Myanmar as the only land bridge to Southeast Asia and beyond and its strategic importance for India's security particularly in the context of the India's northeast. India's northeastern states of Arunachal Pradesh, Nagaland, Manipur and Mizoram share a long land border with Myanmar's states of Kachin, Sagaing and Chin. There exist strong and ethnic kinship and cultural ties between the people living on both sides of the border. The significance of Northeast India has grown over the years because of its land linkages with Myanmar. There have been migrations of people from different parts of Southeast Asia to Assam and the adjoining areas.[6] Prime Minister Modi also spelled out that Myanmar is an important component in India's Act-East Policy when he visited Myanmar.[7] That is why in augmenting the Act-East Policy, the northeast of India emerges, by the criterion of geography, as the region which will act as the strategic catalyst or game changer in accomplishing the vision that the policy aspires to embolden.[8] Befriending Myanmar therefore, offers India to reap the benefits from the consequential transformation of the landlocked northeast to a land-linked one.[9] Only then can geography be used as an opportunity to translate into long-standing trade relations across both land borders and the sea route to assist northeast India to come out from its state of remoteness, underdevelopment and instability.

Although the pattern of India's relation with Myanmar has a direct bearing on security and development of Northeast India, yet it has failed to capitalise on its relations with Myanmar whether economic or strategic or in ensuring energy security. Unable to execute major projects on time, India has lost much ground in Myanmar despite the freedom it has had to deepen commercial ties in these years.

While it is true that India has to act swiftly to fully implement and leverage the existing framework and ensure that it delivers, what has to also be taken heed of is that simply construction of roads will not help connect the two countries unless the issue of security is addressed. More importantly, connectivity is not merely about creating physical infrastructure; it is also about connecting people by reviving shared links. In order to facilitate easy movement of people and allow greater people-to-people contact between the two countries at the level of students, scholars and academic exchanges, the Inner Line Regulation of 1873 and the Restricted Area Permit (RAP) required for foreigners to gain entry to states such as Arunachal Pradesh, etc., must be revoked. Such regulations go against the vision of opening up the northeast India through the Act-East Policy.

India being located between the Golden Crescent in the West and Golden triangle in the East faces the challenge of arms-drugs nexus. It is therefore, equally important to address the issue of smuggling of drugs, goods and arms if India seeks to open Northeast India to the ASEAN countries. Failing which India will not be able to use its eastern frontiers to benefit from the opening up with Myanmar.[10]

What's more important is that India needs to cooperate with Myanmar to ensure the security of the Bay of Bengal and work out mature plans of development especially in stalled projects, and harness the potential for strategic military cooperation that will secure India's northeastern region. India's maritime policy cannot be divorced from its Look/Act East Policy, in which the North-East India factor is an important driver. For instance, the Kaladan multimodal project is intended to provide an outlet to landlocked North-East India into the Indian Ocean (Mizoram in North-East India to Sittwe port in Myanmar). The port connectivity has to be seen in conjunction with road and rail connectivity (the Asian Highway and the Trans-Asian Railway network). Unless these domestic drivers remain untapped it is likely that the policy will continue to have a limited relevance for Northeast India.

The shared ties of the border communities along the India Myanmar border can be used as a link to Southeast Asia given the fact that the ethnic bonds are the oldest connection between India and Myanmar. These communities want greater interaction with Myanmar so that Northeast India can become an integral part of the development along the space connecting the two.[11] Hence, India should begin to take steps to draw advantage from such desire for engagements. A successful Act-East Policy will have to ensure the role played by border communities. Likewise the transnational movement of goods, capital, and labour, cross border exchanges through informal means will need to be studied seriously. This is particularly so when many ordinary citizens (rather than gangsters alone) take advantage of the grey areas in unregulated transactions. The process of this shadow economy, which is a characteristic feature of border economies, will have to be evidenced. Similarly, cross-border transit infrastructure deficits, which are a major drag on India-Myanmar trade, will have to be addressed. In the recent past the two countries have been engaged in contestation over border fencing, fixing and repairs of border pillars and other aspects of border management. Consequently border management remains a critical challenge in the future.

Again it is equally important to bear in mind that Myanmar can attain some form of stability only when it is able to successfully address the ethnic question.[12] This fundamental question needs to be addressed not just for Myanmar but is as important especially in the context of India's northeast which houses more than 200 ethnically, linguistically and culturally distinct groups. Given that both Myanmar and India are faced with the problem of ethnic insurgency it is pertinent to develop a better appreciation of the complex internal dynamics that it generates and the role of democracy in managing them. In a way therefore, Myanmar also holds the key to the ongoing insurgency in the North-East India.

Prime Minister Narendra Modi coined the term natural Economic Zone and called for the northeastern region to be developed through economic corridors to Southeast Asia.[13] Prime Minister Modi had also emphasised on the significance of regional connectivity for economic prosperity during the 12th ASEAN-India Summit.[14] While this may be a promising offer, at the same time, however, it is crucial to undertake an in-depth examination on whether India's conceptualisation of the Act East Policy has any room for the unique local ways of doing trade.[15] Whether they are equipped to handle trade in the context of Look-East Policy/Act East Policy that was essentially crafted within the framework of neo-liberalism? In the tribal societies kinship ties are very strong. Are such ties inimical to the idea of liberating individual entrepreneurial freedoms and skills? Are they then equipped to operate within such parameters? Furthermore, if augmenting development of India's North-East was a key factor of the Look East Policy, have the productive capacities of the region been sufficiently developed to provide a level playing ground in the market relations? What must therefore be ensured is that the pattern of investment and development gives appropriate representation to all sections of the people of the Northeast.[16] Greater participation of the local people in production and distribution activities should be assured. The last but not the least is to confirm that the Northeastern states have adequate representation and taken into confidence or given room to participate in the implementation of the policy.[17]

One more way to enhance the role that Northeast India can play would be to convert Northeast India's history and culture into a soft power resource. The shared heritage between India and the ASEAN region ranging from Borobudor, in Indonesia to Angkor Wat, the world's largest religious monument, in Cambodia, the spread of Indian mythology and folklore, the Thai epic Ramakien based on the Ramayana, etc., are well known and documented. The shared cultural and traditional heritage between India's northeast and the ASEAN countries are yet to be explored. The common food, culture, weaving motifs, hunting practices, etc., in their own unique way can be used as a link to strengthen relations. Another good beginning would be to persuade the new government in Myanmar to allow greater people-to-people contacts between the two countries. There are a sizeable number of people of Indian origin in Myanmar. The potential role that the Indian diaspora can play is yet to be explored. Additionally, it would do well for India to focus on Indian assistance for monuments that reflect the shared history of both countries. Similarly, just as educational Institutions have in the past played an important role where scholars from across Asia came to study in renowned Indian universities such as Nalanda and Takshashila in the present context educational institutions housed in Northeast India can play a very important role. Not simply as nodal points but much more than that. Courses on Southeast Asian history, politics, languages, etc., can be introduced in these universities so that students are exposed to the world of Southeast Asia. For this purpose, teachers specialised in the said areas can be employed to disseminate knowledge about Southeast Asian region with which India is seeking deeper engagement.

While leading the Buddha Purnima prayers in May 2015, Prime Minister Narendra Modi had said that 'the 21st Century will be Asia's century and without Buddha, this cannot be Asia's century.' Clearly Prime Minister Modi's placing of Buddhism at the centre of India's diplomatic initiatives is a creative idea. A high profile Chinese Ambassador, Hu Shih, echoes the image of India as a cradle of wisdom that has given it a unique identity when he had said "India conquered and dominated China culturally for 20 centuries without ever having to send a single soldier across her border."

Northeast India houses many important Buddhist sites and important monasteries. Efforts can be made to derive geopolitical benefits from the Buddhist links to win the hearts of the Buddhist population of Southeast Asia that will entail for enduring relations between the two regions. Once again the path of the Buddha can be traced from Arunachal Pradesh to Myanmar and beyond. India could then utilise the Buddhist heritage circuits, so that there is an increase in the Asian pilgrims annually. This in turn will encourage greater interaction leading to an increase in trade, commerce and tourism in the entire region.[18] Simultaneously, in the tourism sector specifically ecotourism can be promoted. For this to translate to reality two policy goals are currently pertinent. First, there is the need to improve infrastructure, particularly in transportation and the service sector; second, to involve the local people in the activities. The service sector will have to be upgraded keeping in mind the fact that this is a seismic zone and therefore any construction will have to be friendly to the environmental needs. Simple cottages with clean essential facilities for a comfortable break, Internet access and connectivity are the basic requirements that need to be fulfilled, which would attract visitors from not just Southeast Asia but from world over. Needless to say, for this to actually happen air connectivity and roads will have to improve sufficiently. For example, state capitals be connected by direct flight to the capitals of the ASEAN countries together with simplifying travel formalities.

So far India has been unable to meet the expectations of its ASEAN friends who more often than not complain about New Delhi not 'doing enough'. The high level visits to some of the ASEAN countries that the Modi government undertook in a short span of time were meant to signal the shift to the goal of making up the lost ground of implementation of that policy that broadly encompasses the key elements of development of economic relations, strengthening of soft power ties, etc. However, India's Act-East Policy will have to feature Northeast India with a clear roadmap in place. In this India needs to recognise the fact that Myanmar shares a long border with China with which it has long historical association. It would not be in good judgment for the wise elephant to attempt to replace or compete with the mythical dragon. Instead it should explore and work on the areas where it enjoys a distinct edge in Myanmar. However, without a cooperative Myanmar it would be difficult to translate its Look-East policy to Act-East policy in the context of opening continental connections through several points along the 1643 km[18] international border with Myanmar. There is no doubt that Myanmar is an important factor if the Act-East Policy is to live up to its potential of becoming the Northeast's road to peace and prosperity.

ENDNOTES

1. On India's relations with Southeast Asia and its Look East Policy, see Sudhir Devare, 'India & Southeast Asia: Towards Security Convergence', Institute of Southeast Asian Studies, Singapore, 2006; Prakash Nanda, *Rediscovering Asia: Evolution of India's Look East Policy*, Lancer Publisher, New Delhi, 2003; Isabelle Saint-Mezard, *Eastward Bound: India's New Positioning in Asia*, Manohar-CHS, New Delhi, 2006. & P.V. Narasimha Rao, 'India and the Asia Pacific: Forging a New Relationship', Institute of Southeast Asian Studies, Singapore, 1994.
2. Association of Southeast Asian Nations (ASEAN) was established in Bangkok in August 1967. The original members were Indonesia, Malaysia, the Philippines, Singapore and Thailand. Brunei joined in 1984, Vietnam in 1995, Laos and Myanmar in 1997, and Cambodia in 1999.
3. http://www.mea.gov.in/SpeechesStatements.htm?dtl/24238/Prime_Ministers_remarks_at_the_9th_East_asia_Summit_Nay_Pyi_Taw_Myanmar (Accessed on 16 November 2014)
4. Prashanth Parameswaran, "Modi Unveils India's 'Act East Policy' to ASEAN in Myanmar", *The Diplomat*, 17 November 2014.
5. See Graham Lees, "Burma is the Key to India's 'Look East' Economic Strategy', 19 July 2007; available at <http://www.worldpoliticsreview.com/article.aspx?id=941>
6. For more on cross-border history, see Thant Myint-U, *Burma and the New Crossroads of Asia Where China Meets India*, London: Faber and Faber, 2011, pp. 225–47.
7. See Prime Minister Narendra Modi's opening statement at the 12 ASEAN Summit, Myanmar.
8. Namrata Goswami, 'Act East Policy: Northeast India as a Strategic Catalyst', CLAWS Journal l, summer 2015, p. 71.
9. See Munmun Majumdar, 'Engaging Myanmar: Using the North-East India as a Crucible', *International Journal of South Asian Studies*, 6(1), January-June 2013, pp. 118–28.
10. Ibid.
11. See V.S. Seshadri, 'Transforming Connectivity Corridors between India and Myanmar into development Corridors', Research and Information System for Developing Countries-RIS, New Delhi: RIS, 2014.

12. See David I Steinberg, 'Myanmar's Perpetual Dilemma: Ethnicity in a "Discipline-Flourishing Democracy', *Politics, Governance and Security Series*, (22), April 2011, East West Centre Working Paper.
13. Namrata Goswami, op. cit., p. 72.
14. 'Remarks by the PM at the 12th ASEAN-India Summit', Nay Pyi Taw, Myanmar, November 12, 2014 available at http://www.narendramodi.in/remarks-by-the-pm-atthe- 12th-india-asean-summit-nay-pyi-taw-myanmar/
15. 'Barter Trade with Myanmar under the Indo-Myanmar Border Trade Agreement', Reserve Bank of India, October 16, 2000; available at http://rbidocs.rbi.org.in/rdocs/ notification/PDFs/16423.pdf.
16. See Munmun Majumdar, 'Northeast India As a gateway to India's Look East Policy', *International Journal of South Asian Studies*, 1, July-December 2008, pp. 401–2.
17. Speech by the President of India Pranab Mukherjee to the Members of Arunachal Pradesh Legislative Assembly, 29 November 2013, http://presidentofindia.gov.in/sp291113-1.html (Accessed on 1 December 2013).
18. Jarnail Singh, Secretary of the Ministry of Development of Northeast Region, in his speech in the three-day conference organised by the Ministry and Indian Chamber of Commerce, Hanoi, 12 February 2009. See www.saigon-gdaily.com.vn/Business/2009/2/68535/
19. Border Darshan and The Indian Page maintain the length of India-Myanmar boundary as 1643 km with Arunachal Pradesh – 520 km, Manipur – 398 km, Mizoram – 510 km and Nagaland – 215 km at http://archives.is/6kkUu (Accessed on 15 June 2012).

9

Engaging with ASEAN:
Need for a Novel Approach

Sanjeeb Kakoty

The emergence of the modern nation state would undoubtedly rank as one of the major developments in this century. With the emergence of the nation state, what also became sacrosanct was the concept of national boundaries and the principle of its inviolability. In other words, world populations became identified not on the basis of race or language but on the basis of the nation state and free migration of people became anathema to the concept of the state. In the process, groups of people sharing the same race, language or religious belief systems were separated by artificial boundaries created by the new nation states. This phenomenon has led to piquant situations in most parts of the world. For instance, the Indian subcontinent was divided into multiple countries though they shared common ethnic, linguistic or religious ties. On the reverse could be cited the example of the USSR emerging as one country with multiple ethnicities but later breaking up into multiple countries once again!

Thus it is apparent that politics has often undone what history, culture and heritage had long established. Nearer home, one may cite the example of the North Eastern Region of India and the neighbouring countries of East Asia. Over the centuries the valleys and hills of the North-East has attracted migration from different parts of the continent. In time the region emerged as the melting pot of culture, language and civilisation. If one were to look at the different races inhabiting the region, one would find Negritos, Mon Khmers, Tibeto Burmans, Chinese, Shans, Tai, Aryans to name a few and the languages and dialects spoken would be in their mind boggling hundreds.

It is not without a reason that the north-east called the region where India ends and south east Asia begins! It is next to impossible to draw political boundaries that would not transgress upon ethnic, cultural or linguistic ties. In other words, similar ethnic groups live in either side of the border, be it in Bangladesh, Myanmar, China or Bhutan. All these areas that have kindred groups inhabiting it were once part of the larger Indian subcontinent. However, with the partition of the country, the borders were drawn without either logic or public consultation. As a result regions that were linked by history, geography and culture were not only partitioned but also made inaccessible to each other. This created huge social, economic and ecological problems that have remained largely unattended.

This lack of understanding and proper respect for culture, geography and ecology in political decision making is incredibly manifest. To understand this better, one may take the example of the mighty River Brahmaputra that arises in the lofty snow-clad peaks of Tibet drains through two of the most densely populated countries of the region, India and Bangladesh. However, in the absence of clear agreements on the rights of lower riparian states, China has started massive hydrological intervention schemes for not only generating hydro power but also using the waters of the Brahmaputra to irrigate and carry water to its parched regions. The lack of consensus to ensure the ecological sustainability of the region has set alarm bells ringing in both India and Bangladesh. While it is understandable that politically, this may be a difficult area to deal with perhaps the cultural connect that ties the region with the rest of Asia be used as a starting point to start the dialogue on the sharing of the Brahmaputra waters?

The same ties can be explored to draw home the economic logic of promoting closer ties, be it using the sea route through Bangladesh to reach the rest of the world or using the road and rail links through Bangladesh to connect the inaccessible regions of the North-East to the rest of the country, as is the case with Tripura and Bengal. While in return Bangladesh could use the resources and markets of the North-East and also develop and use land routes through North-East to connect with Nepal and Bhutan and vice versa.

The concept of the common economy of not only the SAARC nations but also the rest of the Asian nations would certainly receive a huge boost if the North-East of the country is used as a spring board to connect to the rest of East Asia and the common culture and economic realities would certainly act as the necessary lubricant. The idea would be to build on the exiting cultural and historical relations that exist in the North-East of the country with the rest of Asia and use them to help the political and economic relations between India and the rest of the continent on either a bilateral mode or a multi lateral mode. This would not only increase the understanding between the populations of the nations but also help the government to engage at multiple levels to ensure sustainable and inclusive growth of what constitutes a significant portion of humanity.

To create an engagement at multiple levels, one would do well to borrow a few concepts from modern day management philosophy. The first concept that could come in handy is the concept of systems thinking, wherein all issues are seen through the understanding that every small issue is a part of a larger system. In order to solve a problem or to achieve desirable results, the problem at hand should be seen a subset of a larger set and hence in order to change a subset it may be desirable to take the larger system into active consideration. In this regard, the relation between the North-East of India with the rest of Asia can be seen within the larger subsets consisting of the ecological, cultural, historical, geographical, political and economic subsets. All of these combined can be understood as the system under which the political and economic relationship is but a subset. Without a proper understanding the larger system, seeking to make interventions in particular subsets may provide results that are grossly inadequate. So, a major challenge before academics and policy planners is the need to broaden the canvas to enable a systems approach to problem solving.

Once the holistic lens of the systems approach is adopted, the next challenge would be the create a suitable mechanism that would enable the process of goal setting and realisation of desired results within specific time frames. In the realm of management, this is sought to be achieved through the use of a process called Design Thinking. A combination of Systems Approach and Design Thinking opens up amazing possibilities for reframing and invigorating the existing space and context of intercourse between the North-East and the rest of Asia.

Design Thinking basically rests on the three principles of:

a. Desirability,
b. Feasibility, and
c. Viability.

In other words, any plan of action that is envisaged or any goal that is set has to first pass the test of whether it is desirable in a social, moral and ethical perspective. The next step would be to examine if it is feasible in terms of technology, available manpower etc., and finally, whether it would be financially viable. If in case a result that is sought to be achieved is desirable, but not feasible nor viable, the idea would be have to be reworked upon and suitably modified to ensure both feasibility and viability. Most grandiose plans of regional connectedness and cooperation though desirable, never see the light of day due to the absence of either one or both the factors of feasibility and viability.

It is imperative for academics and specialised institutions like the ASEAN Studies Centre to provide the necessary impetus to look at new concepts that would lay the necessary ground work for policy planners and administrators to initiate path breaking initiatives for regional and sub-regional cooperation. The challenge is, can we do it? Can it be done soon enough?

10

The Act East Policy Implications and Developmental Strategies in Mizoram

K.V. Reddy

At the outset, the main aim of this paper is to study the nature of developmental process in the Northeast Indian state of Mizoram in the post-statehood period. The study is focused on the social, economic, cultural and political perspectives of development in the state. It also tries to identify the problems and prospects in the context of several developmental strategies that were initiated by the central and state governments. The Act East Policy is one such developmental strategy that got contextualised with the development of Northeast Indian state of Mizoram. While the policy was in vogue for over two and half decades, its local implications are hardly satisfactory. Following the change of regime in Delhi and elsewhere in the Myanmar, there are prospects of such policy being implemented well than before.

As usual, developmental process is an ongoing one that witnessed a few ups and downs at various points of time. State and non-state actors have been actively involved in this process of development in the Northeast region. Apparently, there has been significant progress in the region, more so in the state of Mizoram that had been quite peaceful in the post-statehood period. Yet, the state witnessed several setbacks as far as stabilising its economy and social development. Despite many an attainment in the context of certain developmental indicators, the state has had its share of fiascos that could be marked quite conspicuously. As part of examining a few achievements, challenges and drawbacks of the developmental process, an attempt has been made to interact with various stakeholders in the state.

Mainstream Perceptions

Incidentally, the developments in the post-Independence were marked by the rise of separatist tendencies and movements that favoured greater autonomy. In response, the mainstream leadership tried to implement the theory of assimilation and integration in the region. Even some historians considered the NEI as frontier region, and advocated such mainstream policies with the help of which the region could be 'integrated with the mainland' somehow. Some of the national regimes relied excessively on the 'stick and carrot policy' in the initial phases of regional movements. Thus, whenever the military approaches were unsuccessful, the 'Centre started pumping in huge sums of money', neglecting to build the necessary infrastructure.[1] These financial packages and generous funds were considered as counterproductive in a state that deserved communitarian perspective as a way forward towards achieving social development.

In this developmental milieu, Sanjib Barua made a sarcastic comment, 'One idea that enjoys widespread acceptance is that once the problem of the region's economic backwardness is taken care of, the main source of political turmoil will go away'.[2] This sort of highhanded approach had isolated the region and its people beyond any sort of patch-up. Yet, during the course of Constitutional making,[2] Dr. Ambedkar realised the need of keeping its distinct identity intact and thus advocated for conferring the 'special status' (Sixth Schedule) on such regions, for instance. Of course, it has helped the regional states to some extent. Many more such constitutional mechanisms could have been implemented in both letter and spirit, but in vain!

Mizoram Profile

As one of the smallest states in India, Mizoram is an industrially backward state with a vast majority of its people living below the poverty line. Mizoram lacks infrastructures for ensuring economic development. Although agriculture is the primary occupation of its population, the rough and hilly terrain of the state has severely put a limit on the scope of its production capacity. The state has recorded the top rank in the context of literacy levels in the NEI and second rank in the country in the recent past. The state is having a high literacy rate with 91.6%, male 93.7%, and female 89.4%. Given a skill development programme, the state and its literate population could derive lot of benefits in the service sector. Although laudable, its high literacy percentage has significantly contributed for the growth of unemployment in Mizoram. In a way, the state's advantage of high literacy has been viewed as a liability rather than an asset!

Besides, the unique socio-cultural institutions, difficulty and high cost of transport, language barriers has put a constraint upon the local youth to seek employment outside Mizoram. Without the expansion of governmental administration and activities it is unlikely that they would acquire gainful employment. Viewed in this context, efforts of both the state and non-state actors towards developing the state have been quite fruitful. More particularly, it is the Union Government that had changed the very course of developmental paradigm, following the implementation of the Look East Policy in the region. In a way, contextualising the regional development with its frontier policy towards the ASEAN countries including that of Myanmar has certainly enhanced the prospects of the development in the region.

Problematical Issues

Although there are multiple interpretations of development and its various dimensions, this study has focused on the socio-economic development of Mizoram. Theoretically, development can be understood as an organised intervention in collective affairs according to a standard of development. What constitutes development and what it means of appropriate intervention vary in different socio-economic contexts as well as that would be dependent upon specific power relations in a state or society. Thus, it is largely context-specific. And, various actors or stakeholders were expected to play their role during the process of development in the state. More particularly, it is the state and its various governmental agencies that played a leading role, whereas non-state actors like the civil society and NGOs were contributing their mite towards different developmental indicators in their own way, complementary to that of the state.

Also, Mizoram is such a Northeastern state that had been developed on account of equivalent contribution of both state and non-state actors during the period of statehood and after. Thus, this study takes into account various efforts of the state, both state and central governments, besides that of non-state actors like the Church and its affiliated civil society organisations and NGOs in the last two decades or so. As usual, the central government had extended its financial assistance, quite generously (for being declared special category states), to all the Northeastern states including Mizoram for over several decades. Not only was it beneficial to these states to ensure peace and harmony in the region, but also helped them achieve socio-economic development in different sectors over the years. Of all other states, Mizoram has emerged as the most peaceful state in the region, besides contributing to its human development success. Yet, there are several areas that still deserve attention of the state and non-state actors, if the state is to ensure comprehensive development in the days to come.

Expectedly, the state had received a major share of its plan and non-plan outlays from out of the central funding that was largely used for the development of the state. Besides, there were numerous central-government-sponsored schemes that got implemented in the state quite effectively. There has been significant progress in the agricultural development and its allied fields. And, there has been marked improvement in the industrial and infrastructure developments in the field of transportation (surface and airport) and communication systems.[3] Thus, the economic condition of the Mizos, particularly those of the urban areas like Aizawl, Champhai and other towns, has been healthier than that in the pre-statehood period. Obviously, there is an improvement in the basic civic amenities like the primary education, health care, drinking water supply, sanitation among others in the state.

Certainly, industrial activity is yet to take off in the state. Unemployed youth are desperate to secure sustainable jobs in either public or private sectors. There is scope for exploring natural and mineral resources like oil and natural gas and thereby to establish some big power generating industries. Similarly, proper implementation of the Act East Policy (AEP) is possible with contextualising it within the northeast development. Long-pending developmental projects could be undertaken at the earliest so that the state was converted into a real 'gateway' to the Association of South East Asian Nations (ASEAN) and other countries in the East. As part of the state initiatives and governmental responses, both the governments have crucial roles to play in this endeavour.

Although the state government has been responding to the central initiatives and funds quite positively, several projects have not been implemented as per the fixed schedules. Besides sociopolitical factors, local issues have also been attributed for the mismanagement of some sponsored schemes in the state. Similarly, local regimes have also reversed many a development programme on account of political grounds. Suffice it to cite the case of implementing the Anti-jhumming agricultural operation like that of New Land Use Policy (NLUP) during the congress and non-congress regimes in the state on few occasions. Irrespective of change of nomenclature of the programme, this agricultural programme has been criticised for being tainted with corruption and mismanagement in the state.

At the other end, while non-state actors like those belonging to different denominations of the Church were proactive in ensuring peace and social harmony in the state, their scant regard for developmental activities has been noticed in the recent past. Their effective intervention during the course of conducting peaceful elections has always been welcome, that got mass appreciation, but their unsolicited role in certain governmental activities was hardly acceptable. Occasionally, some Church leaders were accused of indulging in non-governmental activities like enforcing the Inner Line Permit (ILP) regulations on few occasions. Political leaderships and the party system in the state were under the grip of some Church denominations and thus failed to deliver goods at times.

Viewed in this perspective, development or otherwise of the state is dependent upon the role that these non-state actors would be playing in the state. Thus, this study has accordingly highlighted the issues and concerns of development, keeping in view the prevalent developmental progress in the state. Besides, the two-decade and half-old Look East Policy (LEP) or the AEP could hardly be implemented since the development of Mizoram was not contextualised with it. To be specific, though the border trade has got lot of potential with establishing the border spot like Zokhawthar (Champhai) on the India-Myanmar route not much was witnessed with regard to developing the local interests.[4]

Perhaps, the proposed ASEAN centre could become a catalyst to promote the trade and development in the NEI and beyond.

Developmental Prospects

The state of Mizoram has been generating rich human resources in terms of educated skilled workers for being employed in the high-profile service sector (public and private jobs) that could contribute more to the state exchequer so that constant dependency on the central funding would be weakened in the days to come. Of course, every government had implemented new socio-economic schemes. Nevertheless the success rate seems to be inadequate. Development still took a heavy toll even though several programmes were undertaken by various governments in the state. Ultimately, the problem lies in the political and administrative systems that need to ensure good governance in bringing out the appropriate developmental works efficiently.

Besides, unlike the mainstream India, this NEI region has an added demographic advantage, due to low density. Christianity and education paved the way for development in Mizoram and play a vital role in all spheres of its lives. Meanwhile, in terms of politics, there are two major political parties (INC and MNF) in Mizoram that dominated the political scenario of the state. Besides an age-old YMA, Mizoram has had a forum called the Mizoram Peoples Forum (MPF), which had acted as a guardian of society and politics in order to have clean and fair governance in the state. Thus, Mizoram has developed a distinct political process that could be effective in ensuring the development of the Mizos. Besides, their fellow-Mizos, cutting across the geographical borders, could also derive the developmental benefits, once the ASEAN countries are brought closer to Mizoram.

'Act East' Implications

Incidentally, the well-being of its people is an important component of human development. Besides economic dimension, educational and health indicators certainly contribute to the human development of the people. Of course, economic development is an important indicator of state development in the country and elsewhere. Agriculture that was once the main economic activity in the state has over the years, had taken a back seat with the service sector becoming the most important sector in terms of contribution to the state income and its welfare. Despite the implementation of New Land Use Policy (NLUP) that was a flagship program of the Congress regimes in the state, its economic performance from the primary sector income was inadequate and limited; the state could achieve better economic performance due to other sectoral improvements.

Universally, the development of infrastructure, particularly transport infrastructure, is a key prerequisite for economic development. However, in Mizoram, the lack of adequate transport infrastructure has been a major inhibiting factor on its economic growth and development. Being a hilly state with difficult terrain and climatic conditions, transport infrastructure in Mizoram is essentially road-based one. While there is a small metre-gauge rail link at Bairabi (about 130 kms from Aizawl) that is to be developed soon,[5] besides an airport at Lengpui (44 kms from Aizawl), for promoting business and personal purposes in Mizoram, road transport is the only principal means of communication. Of course, the state has good potential for economic growth in the areas of agriculture, horticulture, tourism, and handicrafts. Once it is linked with the outside world physically and otherwise, through the LEP/AEP, then there can be better prospects of economic development being secured.

Yet, bad governance has been a major problem in Mizoram and elsewhere in the region.[6] Besides, the region is caught in a vicious cycle of economic backwardness and 'outsider' apprehensions as a result of which developmental initiatives from the private sector are hardly undertaken. Thus it is natural for the local people entertaining a sense of alienation from the mainstream India and feeling of being deserted in the case of developmental activities. Once the process of governance is improved and local population is engaged in the projects that were implemented as part of AEP projects then there would be no looking back as far as development of Mizoram is concerned.

To conclude, in the wake of making it an Act East Policy, certain developmental initiatives on account of the erstwhile LEP have been encouraging, particularly in the second phase of its implementation in the region. Not only that the surface connectivity between the region and the ASEAN countries could be established, but people-to-people connectivity could also be strengthened with regard to the Myanmar. With the increase in the border trade and boosting of tourist potential, these northeastern regional states would become ultimate beneficiaries. While the non-state actors and their various agencies are actively engaged in the process of peace and development, union-state governments can elevate the level of development beyond anybody's expectations. Perhaps, the case of ASEAN-Northeast Indian relationship could offer multiple advantages to the state of Mizoram and its neighbours.

ENDNOTES

1. Misra Udayon, *Quest for Identity*, Guwahati: Omsons Publications, 1988.
2. Ambedkar, BR., 1950. Constituent Assembly Debates vol. IX.
3. Satpathy RK, 'Contextualising Development in The-state-Civil Society Paradigm of Mizoram', in the Edited volume by JK Patnaik, 'Peace and Development in Mizoram – role of the state and civil society' (Department of Political Science, Mizoram university, Aizawl, 2008), p.124.
4. Unlike the case of Moreh (Manipur), the Mizoram border spot was hardly developed infrastructure-wise or otherwise, as was observed by the author as part of his field study last year.
5. *The Mizoram Post*, May 28, 2016.
6. Reddy, K.V., 'State, Governance and Development in Northeast India—Emerging Challenges in Mizoram', in *State and Participatory Governance in Northeast India* Lalneihzovi (ed.), New Delhi: Mittal Publications, 2016.

11

Role of Culture in Activation of the Act East Policy

P.P. Shrivastav

The Dynamic Act East Policy

The two words *Act East* themselves clarify the intention behind the policy decision announced by our Prime Minister, Shri Narendra Modi, at the 12th ASEAN-India Summit and East Asia Summit (Naypyidaw, Myanmar: Nov 2014). It was about injecting dynamism into the earlier *LOOK EAST Policy* of the 90s and transforming it into action-oriented *ACT EAST Policy*. Of particular interest, he added, was the issue of enhancing connectivity between India and ASEAN, not just by land and sea, but also by air. Moreover, institutional, digital and people-to-people connectivity were no less important. He also highlighted the importance of measures which could yield rich dividends, like free movement of people, particularly professionals; creation of regional value chains to increase economic interdependence for mutual benefit; recognition of each other's educational qualifications and degree, and the likes. This has opened a bright vista of opportunity for prosperity and progress for the people in our North Eastern States, India's land-bridge to our Eastern neighbours.

Without going into details of the specific schemes approved and in the pipeline, and their progress on the ground, let us discuss the deep significance of culture in the context of the process—earlier of *looking East* and now of *acting East*—and in making it meaningful to the people in a manner that touches their heart, makes them partners in its implementation and enables them to derive full benefits of peace, prosperity and progress from it.

The common grievance shared by the people of our North Eastern Region has been that of isolation and backwardness. Allegations of neglect are levelled mainly against the *Central Government* as if it is insensitive being far from the periphery.[1] It will, therefore, be pertinent to examine when and how such feelings arose and who (Union, State or Local Government) has failed to take action; and to identify the *way forward for their redressal.*

Coming to the ground realities in the context of the grievance of *isolation,* the fact is that right from the ancient BC era, there was plenty of socio-economic and cultural interaction among the peoples inhabiting the vast command area of the mighty Ganga-Brahmaputra-Meghna-Irrawady-Mekong River systems and beyond the Indonesian Islands. This is supported by references in our mythology and epics and in the striking cultural similarities among the peoples. In the words of an eminent historian, *"Most striking, however, are finds from excavation in the Assam Garo Hills border dated to 1000 BCE, that show culture closely linked with Southeast Asia."*[2] People could move freely all over and be understood by each other. The role of Indian scholars, artists, artisan and traders led to symbiotic exchange of knowledge, culture and skills leading to economic prosperity for all. Some of the finest ships were built by the coastal communities in Bengal. Trade flourished not only from our Eastern Coast but also from as far as Gujarat on the

Western Coast. It is through such P-2-P (People-to-People) contacts and interactions at various levels that the highly developed Indian culture got adopted and adapted across this vast region. This was an entirely voluntary process free from coercion or force.

In the words of the well-known historian, Prof. Romilla Thapar, 'Sanskrit influenced the languages of elite cultures, probably because it was the language of the formal rituals introduced by Indian functionaries. Some of the finest Sanskrit inscriptions came from these areas. Geographical place-names associated with Indian tradition were adopted; for example, Authia the ancient capital of Thailand, was named after Ayodhya, the capital of the kingdom of Rama, this being one among many instances of the popularity of the Indian epics. Indian iconographic norms were fused with local forms in the images. The particular style of intertwining Buddhism and the Puranic religion, so representative of sites in Southeast Asia, evolved later in its most creative forms at Angkor Vat and the Bayon in Cambodia, and the stepped stupa at Borobudur and the Prambanan temple, both in Java.' The Indian impact is understandable, she goes on to say, 'in terms of certain advanced technologies arriving in the area and the local elite adopting new patterns. The process of Indian traders also assisted the change, introducing an exchange economy that benefitted them and allowed them to participate at various levels of power ....The local culture was visible in all aspects of life.' That is how Hinduism, Buddhism and later Islam also came from the Indian side and all these faiths have coexisted peacefully so far.

This happy state of affairs was rudely shattered around the 15th century when European Powers came in and using temptation, deception, coercion and force, started the process of fragmentation and colonisation. Six or so centuries later, fighting broke out in Europe itself involving the colonial powers and the two World Wars created conditions that led to end of their colonisation and to emergence of a number of politically independent self-ruled nation-States in Asia.

The colonial administration, interested more in revenue-generation from the new industries based on Tea, Coal and Oil in Assam, brought in the Inner Line Regulations primarily to keep the hill tribes out to ensure safety for their trade and commerce in the vast Assam plains. This, added to the normal problems of communications in hilly terrain, did lead to feeling of isolation among the hill-people. Partition of the country in 1947, with the ill-conceived and mischievous Durand Line lacerating Bengal and cutting off the established surface-route communication links between the North Eastern Region and the rest of India, added to the problem. Only a narrow strip of land, like the proverbial *chicken's neck*, remained. With a National Highway and a Railway Line, it now provides the land-link to the rest of the country. This bottleneck also contributes to the feeling of isolation and backwardness.

Reverting now to the slow but powerful and abiding influence of Nature on man, the warm salubrious climate of the Ganga-Brahmaputra-Meghna-Irrawady-Mekong River Basin played the major role in shaping the body and mind, lifestyle and habits, thinking and mindset, culture and civilisation of the peoples. The rich, largely common, culture with strong local flavours and features, which emerged in this large S-E Asian region, represented a quantum jump in cultural and spiritual evolution of man. Thinkers in this culture, especially in India, concentrated their attention within and started their quest for knowledge from the subtle to the gross—from the nature of *Self* and the *Primordial Creative Principle* of the entire Creation, call it Ishwar in Sanskrit, God in English, or by any other name. By getting in tune with this principle one could gain knowledge, internally through intuition, of everything else in the universe which is but the manifestation of this all-pervading One. With higher degree of such tuning-in, one could make things happen through internal exercise of thought-power and will-power, just as a Scientist can get things done through external means and instruments. Giving primacy to this subtle-most Spiritual dimension of man, they could understand the process of evolution through the principle of eternal conflict between the ever growing negative (aasurik) and positive (daivik) forces. The former, better united, organised and commanded like the military, and the later used unethical means, fair and foul, win the initial battle. But that also raises their negativity in the form of greed and ego and that leads to defeat at the hands of the positive forces with abiding faith in higher values like truthfulness, honesty and righteousness, when they decide to regroup fight with faith and determination. The history of this large S-E Asian belt with happy prosperity, followed by colonisation and then freedom again after half a millennium also points to a long future of peace, prosperity and progress.

Such is the common cultural heritage that India and the ASEAN countries have been sharing since ages, believing in the principle of universal brotherhood (*Vasudhaiva Kutumbakam,* in Sanskrit, meaning that the *entire universe is but one family*). Our shared culture believes in adopting and adapting all that is best from everywhere and thus provides the fertile soil on which symbiotic people-oriented programmes of collective peace, prosperity and progress have been growing, blooming, flowering and yielding sweet fruits of happiness for all over the ages.

On the other hand the geo-climatic conditions in the West made the thinkers take the opposite direction, starting from the gross material world outside and proceed towards the subtle. Tremendous progress was made in the West in gaining knowledge of the gross material world through the instrumentality of Science and Technology and they achieved admirable heights of prosperity for themselves. Alongside, however, the play of negative forces of ego and greed led them to colonise the peaceful and trusting peoples in Asia and Africa. The rising graph of their power and prosperity continued for a few centuries till the negativity caught up and led to internecine clashes among themselves. The worst bloodshed that the world had ever seen followed in the form of two World Wars. That led to their withdrawal overtly at least, and we regained our freedom.

The trend in the future is not difficult to guess. The curve of the materialistic culture of the West has passed its zenith and the downward trend has commenced. Also, after long dominance of the physical and then the intellectual power, now time has come for rise of the spiritually oriented culture of the East. Great selfless thinkers and seers like Swami Vivekananda had foreseen and clearly foretold (while returning from the West shortly before 1900) that India would gain independence within 50 years in *unusual circumstances* (which came true in 1947) and also about the Asian-Resurgence, which is coming now. The rise in the curve of Asia began with the independence of India and the other nations of Southeast Asia. The imprint of the Western culture has no doubt penetrated deep, but the deeper abiding value-based cultural-core within us all, has to prevail to protect us against downfall. The time for Asian resurgence has come and we all, especially the youth, have to seize this opportunity and remain at the crest of the wave. Those who fail to rise to the occasion will get swept into stagnating backwaters of progress and of history.

Our common shared cultural background will guide us towards the right Way-Forward to reach the destinations of Peace, Prosperity and Progress for all of us belonging to the South-East Asian brotherhood of peoples inhabiting the vast fertile regions irrigated by the mighty River systems of Ganga-Brahmaputra-Meghna-Irrawady-Mekong and beyond.

The Governments (in the First Space at the top) have already taken the initiative by coming together in groupings like ASEAN, etc. Big Business (in the Second Space) is bound to follow with rise of prosperity through international trade, commerce and industry. It is now for the large Third Space of the People to prepare itself to derive the maximum from these developments. The prime initial need, however, is that of informed awareness of the opportunities that will open up with improved physical connectivity by land, air, rivers, sea; cyber-links by IT; and enhanced socio-economic intercourse among the nations in the ASEAN and even beyond. One way of starting off the people-to-people contacts, especially in border-areas, may be to organise fairs and festivals, games and sports, discussions and debates; where producers and consumers from different areas could exchange knowledge & skills, production costs & sale prices, deficits & surpluses, and the likes. Such occasions could be utilised to organise awareness campaigns as well.

In fact, this process was kick-started jointly by the *Indian Council of World Affairs* (an institution of high repute sponsored by the Government of India in the Ministry of External Affairs) and the Shillong based *Asian Confluence* (*a Civil Society* non-profit organisation devoted to the cause of restoring the age-old cultural unity of this SE Asian region, facilitating confluence of the commonalities of the various cultural streams into a common Asian stream; to end the feeling of isolation and backwardness and bring benefits to all including our people in our NE Region which is the land-bridge between India and our neighbours.

The process was kick-started by The *Shillong Dialogue* (Shillong: Dec 2014) with our immediate neighbours (Bangladesh, Myanmar, Bhutan and Nepal), organised jointly by Asian Confluence and ICWA. It proved an unqualified success and what emerged was the *Shillong Consensus*, the unanimous common approach to improving people-to-people relations. The latest mega-event in this context was the largely attended Asian Confluence River Festival: *NADI-2016* (Shillong: 15-16 July 2016) organised jointly by the Government of Meghalaya, the North Eastern Council and the *Asian Confluence*. In between, an exercise was done at the intellectual by motivating young scholars and researchers to come together for introspection on the contours of a smooth, obstacle-free Road Ahead to prosperity and progress for our people, taking advantage of the Act East Policy initiative and our own locational advantage vis-à-vis the ASEAN neighbourhood. Our youthful scholars and thinkers, under the aegis of *Young Scholars Forum (YSF)* set up jointly by Asian Confluence (AsCon) and the Indian Council of World Affairs (ICWA) as a follow-up of the Shillong Consensus. YSF in its Conclave (Shillong: Dec 20115). came out with a brilliant set of consensus-recommendations. It is reproduced below. See how beautifully YSF has visualised the Way Forward for Peace, Prosperity and Progress for All and recommended the following three parallel Highways, each with its specific milestones:

(i) ***P-2-P Connectivity Highway*** with the following milestones:

- (a) *Physical:* Road/Rail/Air linkages to be developed through G-2-G contacts.
- (b) *Intellectual:* Linkages among Scholars, Academia, Universities, Researchers, Professionals and Institutions.
- (c) *Spiritual:* Heritage/Spiritual Tourism, Fairs & Festivals; Inter-faith Discourses, etc.

(ii) ***Prosperity Highway*** with the following milestones:

- (a) Trade & Commerce
- (b) Tourism
- (c) *Capacity Building:* Knowledge and Skills for *Value addition of local produce* locally.

(iii) ***Progress Highway*** with the following milestones:

- (a) *Governance:* Transparency, Awareness & Stakeholdership of Citizens in Development
- (b) *Introspection:* Identification of own shortcomings and steps to overcome the same
- (c) *Border Management:* Advocate concept of primacy to Human Security in Border Security
- (d) *Climate Change:* Concrete Plans of Awareness, Prevention, Early Warning and Mitigation of natural disasters
- (e) *Setting up of South Asia Centre in NEHU, Shillong*

(f) Periodic holding of such Conclaves in association with Institutions of repute

One of the most effective and convenient ways to achieve the main objective of close P-2-P contacts would be to have a hostel for 100-150 in NEHU for Post Graduate and Research Scholars from ASEAN and other selected countries. Here they could have the type of food that they are used to at home. The ASEAN Centre located in the common campus, could organise Bharat-darshan tours, and visits to other Universities in the NE-Region and other regions of the country as a process of familiarisation with the common cultural heritage. They could make comparative study of rural areas and relevant policies and programmes of rural development in India and those in their own countries and come up with relevant and fresh suggestions. Contact may be maintained with them even after the scholars went back after completing their studies in India. Similar reciprocal arrangements for Indian students could be suggested to the Governments of ASEAN countries and others. This would be a way ahead for a life-long association of India with its neighbouring countries and vice versa.

We would very strongly recommend this measure to build a cadre of motivated scholars who will sustain the laudable movement to build cultural and emotional bridges to bring and keep the peoples of Southeast Asian Region together for mutual peace, prosperity and progress. We are confident that the North-Eastern Hill University in Shillong will welcome such a decision and also start new courses and programmes that will be relevant to the region and to the liking of the guest scholars and researchers from our neighbouring nations. We look forward to the ASEAN Studies Centre at the ICSSR-NERC and NEHU designing a fine super-structure of peace, prosperity and progress on the strong age-old foundations of cultural commonality among the nations in the South-East Asian region.

ENDNOTES

1. The fact is that there is nothing like 'Central' and 'Peripheral' in the system of governance in India since independence. Ours is a fully democratic system of duly elected Union Government, State Governments and Local Authorities as partners in governance with clearly defined functions, powers and resources. Public insistence should rightly be placed on making each of them act properly, instead of resorting to political blame-game of keeping issues alive. There should be pro-active initiatives for solution of the problems in the way.
2. All quotations are from a recent article 'Between the Ganga and the Mekong' written by Prof Imdad Hussain, formerly, Professor of History, North-Eastern Hill University, Shillong.

12

Closing the Chasm:

India's Transition from Looking East to Acting East

Konthoujam Sarda

Introduction

Historical and cultural links between India and Southeast Asia dates back centuries. Indian merchants began bringing Hinduism and Buddhism across the sea by the first century AD, influencing the development of kingdoms and empires such as *Srivijaya* in Sumatra and the *Majapahit* in Java, Bali and the Philippine archipelago (Hall, 1964). Ancient Indian classical works such as the *Ramayana* also makes references to Southeast Asia.

India and ASEAN have committed to intensify efforts to safeguard the symbols and structures representing civilisational bonds between ASEAN and India, which include Angkor Wat in Cambodia, Borobudur and Prambanan temples Indonesia, Wat Phu in Laos, Bagan in Myanmar, Sukhothai Historical Park in Thailand, and My Son Sanctuary in Vietnam.[1]

Ideological differences had precluded close political ties from developing between India and the Southeast Asian countries during the Cold War period. India's balance of payment crisis and subsequent economic liberalisation, coupled with the collapse of the former Union of Soviet Socialist Republic (USSR) and ASEAN's success as a model for regional cooperation as opposed to South Asian Association for Regional Cooperation (SAARC) forced New Delhi's attention toward Southeast Asia via its Look East Policy (LEP) under then Indian Prime Minister Narasimha Rao (Kuppuswamy, 2010).

The ASEAN states were openly supportive of the opening up of India's economy. India was looking for new markets and considering the geographical proximity between India and Southeast Asian countries, economic engagement was a huge opportunity. The use of 'Look East' Policy by the Rao government in 1990 was multi-faceted which had strategic, economic and cultural elements.

The focus of India's Look East Policy in the first phase was to forge closer economic ties with ASEAN member states. It is well known that India became a Sectoral Dialogue Partner in March 1993, a Full Dialogue Partner in 1995, a member of the ASEAN Regional Forum in July 1996 and finally a Summit Level Partner in 2002. It is said that the second phase of the then India's Look East and the now renamed Act East began in 2003 is more comprehensive in its coverage, extending from Australia to East Asia, with ASEAN as its core (Mohan, 2003). This transformation was lucidly underlined by the then External Affairs Minister, Mr Yashwant Sinha, in his speech, 'Resurgent India in Asia', at Harvard University, on September 29, 2003, where he described this new phase as a shift from trade to wider security issues.

The expansion of India's relations with the region can be very well gauged from the fact that trade between India and ASEAN multiplied fourfold—from US$ 3.1 billion in 1991 to US$ 45 billion in 2010-11 to US$ 65.4 billion in the year 2015–16. To boost trade ties further, ASEAN-India Free Trade Agreement (FTA) in goods with the ten members of ASEAN came into force in 1st January 2010. India has formally signed FTA in services and investments in the year 2014 and this is expected to boost India's balance of trade which is currently in ASEAN's favour. India and ASEAN now have 26 annual dialogue mechanisms with ASEAN and sectoral dialogues at Ministerial level in agriculture, commerce, environment, foreign affairs, renewable energy, telecommunications and tourism.

The ASEAN-India Vision Statement 2020 drafted by ASEAN-India Eminent Persons Group on the commemoration of 10th ASEAN-India summit level partnership and upgrading of their relationship to strategic partnership in 2012, committed both the sides 'to fostering greater security cooperation to further address traditional and nontraditional security challenges' including transnational crimes and international terrorism.[2] It further emphasised that leaders of the 11 countries are committed to 'strengthening cooperation to ensure maritime security, freedom of navigation and safety of sea lanes for unfettered movement of trade in accordance with international law'.

India and ASEAN seem to be reorienting their partnership to accommodate the changing geo-strategic factors and demands of geo-politics concerning US's rebalancing its position in Asia and China's growing assertiveness. China's assertive stance in South China Sea has given India the opportunity to enhance strategically with ASEAN, and ASEAN is increasingly looking to India to play a balancing role in the region. The China-ASEAN stand-off over the South China Sea can be said to have led to increased American diplomacy in Southeast Asia. The recent rebranding of India's Look East Policy to Act East Policy is oriented towards enhancing trade, connectivity and India's maritime diplomacy with ASEAN. The then Secretary of States Hillary Clinton in her address in the Indian city of Chennai in the year 2012 urged India to 'not just Look East, but to Engage East and Act East', and months after, the then President of the United States Barack Obama in his address to the Australian Parliament in November 2011 announced that the Asia Pacific will be the top foreign policy priority which later came to be known as US' Asia Pivot Policy.

This paper links China as a common factor in US–India–ASEAN's triangular relations and points out that determining the pace of the India-ASEAN relations largely rest on India strategic vision, especially at a time when ASEAN countries are increasingly wanting India's support in stabilising and shaping the regional economic and security architecture. India's rebranding of its Look East into Act East Policy could be seen as a response towards these developments in the region. ASEAN in calling for stronger strategic ties, acknowledged India's role in ensuring regional peace and stability 'through India's accession to the Treaty of Amity and Cooperation in Southeast Asia (TAC) in 2003 and India's contribution in the ASEAN+1, the ASEAN Regional Forum (ARF), the East Asia Summit (EAS) and the ASEAN Defence Ministers' Meeting (ADMM) Plus'.[3]

China as a Factor in the US-India-ASEAN Relations

Even though Asia is poised to be the centre of world trade and politics, so much so that 21st century is called the Asian Century (The Asian Century: Reality or Hype? 2013), the US rebalancing towards Asia strategy and consequent Chinese responses is referred to as the 'New Great Game' with an East Asia twist and is said to have further implications for global and regional politics (Kassim, 2012). The US rebalancing its position in Asia and China's growing assertiveness constructs a complex scenario for India and ASEAN. This could be seen in the Annual Regional Ministerial meeting at Phnom Pehn in July 2012 where ASEAN could not come up with a joint declaration over the issue of South China Sea. India urged both countries to exercise restraint and resolve the issue diplomatically according to principles of international law (PTI, 2012).

The Philippines, Thailand and Vietnam have welcomed the US repositioning in Asia; countries such as Indonesia and Malaysia have given measured response (Eliot School of International Affairs report, 2014). It is well known at Southeast Asian countries, which are in direct territorial conflict with China, having been doubtful of China's regional aspirations. Though it has been in ASEAN's interest to position itself at the centre of Asian integration through East Asia Summit, ASEAN Regional Forum, ASEAN Defence Ministers Meeting Plus, and ASEAN has not faced a dilemma before of this intensity in accommodating big powers.

It has been debated that India is in a unique position of being wooed by both the US and China (Sandy, 2012). India does not want to disrupt the balance of power in the region by playing a third wheel to the power tussle between US and China to gain regional supremacy. The United States has been also been making efforts to position India as an important strategic partner in Asia. For example, India and the US recently signed a 10-year defence agreement framework on June 3, 2012.

The US's policy towards China has been two fold. Assuming China will continue to rise economically, China could choose to become a responsible power or it could become a rival and aggressor in Asia, therefore the US engagement with China seem to be to increase its stake in the international system while balancing its growing power (Blackwill, Tellis 2015).

What has been happening in the region today is partly because of transfer of U.S. military resources to the Pacific, which has been countered, however, by China's rapid military buildup, and the cycle going back and forth which may have led to China militarising South China Sea and the US taking further defensive measures.

For India stakes in the South China Sea issue are mainly because of three reasons. Firstly, almost one-third of India's trade was with economies in East Asia and more than half of India's trade (55%) with the Asia-Pacific is conducted through the South China Sea (Singh, 2011).

Secondly, the proposed Chinese Maritime Silk Route from the southern China's ports to South China Sea, the Straits of Malacca, to Indian Ocean to the Persian Gulf, Red Sea and Gulf of Aden.[4] It encompasses Asia, the Middle East, East Africa and Europe. It also implies shrinking India's strategic space. On the other hand, China seems to be attempting to monopolise the South China Sea. China is also allegedly encircling India with its String of Pearls Policy. Thirdly, India and ASEAN are thriving trade partners with trade expected to grow remarkably to more than 200 billon dollars in the post-ASEAN Economic Community era (Standard Charter report, 2015).

India-ASEAN Connectivity and Trade

More than two decades after India launched its Look East Policy in 1991, trade between India and ASEAN increased—from US$ 3.1 billion in 1991 to US$ 45 billion in 2010–11 and ASEAN-India trade grew at over 22 percent annually during the 2005–11 (Keck, 2012).

The ASEAN Economic Community (AEC) as a single market and production base has a combined Gross Domestic Product (GDP) values of $2.4 trillion as against India's GDP of around $2 trillion and China's around $9.96 trillion.

In 2016–17 the World Economic Forum in its Global Competitiveness Index Report places India in the 68th position (out of a total sample of 138 countries) when competitiveness is measured in terms of infrastructure development (World Economic Forum, 2013). The report also cited lack of infrastructure as the key bottleneck for global business. The Modi government has advocated a 'Look East, Link West Policy' pointing to a broader Indo-Pacific conceptualisation of India's region. To become part of ASEAN production network, it is necessary for India to have a well-functioning infrastructure to aid economic development to be in tune with Modi's 'Make in India Policy' of making India a manufacturing hub. Besides, when the Modi government came to power in 2014, his priority seemed to be a commitment for fostering stronger relations in the South Asian neighbourhood, but it did not come at the expense of its engagement with its Southeast Asian neighbours.

Border trade between India (through the north-eastern states) and CLMV countries (through Myanmar) is said to have a trade potential of US$10 to US$ 22 million (Export Import Bank of India, 2013). Potential for trade and investment between India and the CLMV countries includes skill development, agricultural products, manufacturing, project exports, energy among others, and culture, connectivity and commerce seem to be the focus of India's engagement with the CLMV countries, with the north-eastern part of India acting as the gateway to north-east India (Business Standard, 2014). India's north-eastern states share a land border of around 1700 kms with Myanmar which is critical to connectivity with Southeast Asia.

It is also important to note that the Prime Minister of India has stressed the importance of India's north-eastern states to be the gateway to the Southeast Asian countries. At the India-ASEAN Summit in Kuala Lumpur in November 2015, Modi announced a Line of Credit of US$1 billion to promote projects that support physical and cultural connectivity between India and ASEAN which signalled the primacy of 'connectivity, culture and commerce'.

It was the for the first time that in the Delhi Dialogue VII Ministerial Session which was held on 18th February 2015 that the Chief Ministers of the North-Eastern States and the ASEAN Ministers participated in a panel discussion on 'Connectivity: Creating Pathways to a Shared Future'.

A three-day business summit of the North-east India and ASEAN Business Summit was held for the first time in Manipur in April 2016 with focus on road connectivity, trade and tourism (IANS, 2016).

North-east India is poised to benefit from India's growing relations with Southeast Asia especially the CLMV countries considering the geographical proximity. However, India's 'Look East' Policy has been largely conceptualised with the sudden demise of the Soviet Union; the policy was originally crafted more as a response by India to the systemic changes in international politics rather than a policy aimed primarily at uplifting its rather backward North-eastern region. It is important to note that once it was realised around 2000 that the 'Look East' Policy was a viable way to develop the North-east; policy/decision makers started arguing for a proactive engagement of North-east India with Southeast Asia (Goswami, 2009).

The north-eastern states that are landlocked have lagged behind the rest of the country in terms of infrastructure and industrial development. Improved transport links via road and river will immensely increase Indian exports into ASEAN in the next 10 years. India's export potential include petroleum products, organic chemicals, vehicles (including auto parts), pharmaceuticals, gems and jewellery, and apparel and clothing accessories (Standard Charter Report, 2014).

India and ASEAN connectivity projects include connecting India-Myanmar-Lao PDR-Viet Nam-Cambodia as well as developing the Mekong-India Economic Corridor (MIEC) connecting Southeast Asia to South Asia (ADBI, 2014). Economic growth and heightened economic engagement with ASEAN will help India solidify its position in the changing regional economic and security scenario.

India' Maritime Pursuits

Post-India and ASEAN upgrading their relationship to strategic partnership in 2012 and with the Modi government coming to power in 2014, India is seen to be focused on greater maritime involvement with other regional maritime powers. In 2014, The Indian Navy has participated in a series of engagements namely PLA-N at Qingdao, the US-led Rim of the Pacific (RIMPAC) exercises, and the US-India MALABAR exercises which Japan joined for the first time.

Apart from stationing a Very Low Frequency (VLF) transmitting station for securing fleet communications with Indian submarines, at the Indian Naval Station Kattaboman in Tamil Nadu (PTI, 2014), the Information Management and Analysis Centre (IMAC) stationed at Gurgaon will track ships in India's territorial waters in the Indian Ocean (Peri, 2014). India also recently held the first Indian Ocean Dialogue under the realm of IORA at Cochin in 2014. Indian Ocean Dialogue aims to serve as a valued and productive platform for the exchange of ideas, concerns and experiences of IORA Member States and would help evolve a common understanding to address challenges in the region. In the inaugural address of Indian Ocean Dialogue, Indian Ambassador Rajiv K. Bhatia said, 'In India's strategic thinking a notion like, sea blindness has no place whatsoever today. Indeed, this Dialogue is a testimony to it' (MEA Speeches, 2014). To compound the importance of the SLOCs, it must be remembered that India imports 70% of its oil requirement through the sea (Institute for the Analysis of Global Security report, 2011). While, recognising the importance of trade, and the volume of trade that is conducted through the sea, only 15% of the defence budget is spent on the Navy (IDSA Report, 2014).

Even though the Andaman and Nicobar Command serves as the locus for India's engagement with regional navies in Southeast Asia which includes bi-annual joint exercises with the navies of Thailand and Indonesia, the annual SIMBEX maritime exercises with Singapore, and the biennial Milan multilateral naval exercises (Smith, 2014).

Even though India's Look East Policy had a strategic component, it is only in the recent past that India chose to heighten its naval diplomacy with Modi government hinting at pursuing a more intense naval diplomacy (Cronin and Baruah, 2015).

In terms of Naval diplomacy, even though India has signalled a heightened naval engagement with individual regional navies it chose to treat its naval engagement with the regional powers as isolated engagements, without giving a strategic shape to it, hence it does not send out a clear strategic message to its regional naval partners as yet. Nevertheless, India seems to be showing an increasing willingness to engage in the larger collective framework, which include countries such as the US, Japan, China, Australia and ASEAN. India is also to manoeuvre its away to accommodate China, which is India's largest trading partner. China remains concerned with India's engagement with its close ally Vietnam, as Vietnam's wants to open Cam Ranh Bay for all the world's navies. India and ASEAN have a common interest in freedom of navigation and free flow of trade, and for New Delhi a degree of ambiguity in its strategic vision has been serving its interest and India may continue to do so.

Conclusion

The developments which has China and the US competing for regional supremacy, and the US nudging India to play a greater role in shaping the regional economic and security architecture have been a factor in India rebranding its Look East into Act East. In the domestic front the Act East Policy is also pronounced in incorporating the North-East of India to be the gateway to Southeast Asia through connectivity and infrastructural development. India's engagement with ASEAN has evolved to be more significant with the changing economic and security architecture constructed with US-China competition in the region.

This can be seen in the India's enhanced maritime pursuits, connectivity and trade, traditional and non-traditional security co-operation. This is long overdue considering the Southeast Asian neighbours have always looked upon India as a balancer to an aggressive China. This gives an opportunity for both India and ASEAN to work in tandem in shaping a peaceful regional economic and security architecture.

ENDNOTES

1. Vision Statement India-ASEAN Commemorative Summit.
2. Vision Statement ASEAN India Commemorative Summit.

REFERENCES

Singh, Amit. *'South China Sea Dispute and India'*. SAEA Group Research, 25 September 2011. Available at http://saeagroup.com/articles/2011/sept/south-china-sea-dispute-and-india.html, Accessed 29 May 2015.

Australian Government Media Release. 2015. Available at http://news.defence.gov.au/2015/06/04/indian-navy-crosses-oceans-to-visit-australia/, Accessed on 25 May 2015.

Blackwill, R.D. & Ashley J. Tellis, *'Revising U.S. Grand Strategy Toward China'*. Council Special Report No. 72, 2015.

Kuppuswamy, C.S., 'India's Look East Policy: A Review'. *South Asia Analysis Group* 3662 (16), 2010.

Chari, P.R. 2012. *'Antony and Panetta: A Shakespearean Drama'*. Available atwww.ipcs.org/.../antony-and-panetta-a-shakespearean-drama-3634.html, Accessed on 25 July 2014.

Cronin M Patrick, Baruah M Darshana, 'The Modi Doctrine for the Indo-Pacific Maritime Region', Available at http://thediplomat.com/2014/12/the-modi-doctrine-for-the-indo-pacific-maritime-region/, Accessed on 5 April 2015.

Export-Import Bank of India Report, India's Trade and Investment Relations with Cambodia , Lao PDR, Myanmar, Vietnam (CLMV). Occasional paper no. 161, 2013.

Gordon, Sandy, 'India: Which Way Will the Swing State Swing', *East Asia Forum*, 2012, Accessed 12 June 2015.

Goswami, Namrata, 'Looking East through India's North-East'. IDSA Occasional Paper No. 2 June 2009. Institute for Defence Studies and Analyses. New Delhi

Hall D.G.E., *A History of Southeast Asia*, London: Macmillan & Co. Ltd, 2010.

IANS. 2016. 'ASEAN-Northeast India business summit opens'.

Institute for the Analysis of Global Security report. 2011. Available at http://www.iags.org/n0121043.htm

Institute of Defence Studies report. 2014. Available at http://www.idsa.in/idsacomments/IndiasInterimDefenceBudget2014-15_lkbehera_230214.html. Accessed on 5 April 2015.

Kassim Razali Yang,, 'The New Great Game: ASEAN's Balancing Act? *RSIS Commentaries*, 2012 Available at http://www.rsis.edu.sg/publications/Perspective/, accessed 16 June, 2014. Accessed on 26 December 2015.

Keck. Z., 'India-ASEAN Celebrate 20th Anniversary with Two FTAs,' *Indian Express*, dated December 21, 2012.

Live Mint. 2013. 'Myanmar gets set to enter world stage at WEF on East Asia'. Available at http://www.livemint.com/Politics/xjK48oTN8yvqJ8sj0tJuwJ/Myanmar-gets-set-to-enter-world-stage-at-WEF-on-East-Asia.html. Accessed 5 May 2014.

Mary Carras, 'The Impact of Chinese Maritime Policies on India'. *Foreign Policy in*

Focus, 2014. *Available at* http://fpif.org/impact-chinese maritime-policies-india. Accessed on 23 August 2014.

Ministry of External Affairs Speeches. 2014. Available at http://mea.gov.in/Speeches-Statements.htm?dtl/23983/Secretary_ERampDPAs_address_at_the_first_ Indian_Ocean_Dialogue_held_under_the_Indian_Ocean_Rim_Association_IORA_ at_Kochi

Osburn, K., 'Congress Seeks to Arm U.S. Allies in the Pacific to Counter China', *Online Defense and Acquisition Journal*, 2015, http://www.dodbuzz.com/2015/05/28/congress-seeks-to-arm-u-s-allies-in-the-pacific-to-counter-china/ Accessed 13 May 2015.

Parameswaran, Prashanth, 'India, Australia, Japan Hold First Ever Trilateral Dialogue'. *The Diplomat*, 2015. Available at http://thediplomat.com/2015/06/india-australia-japan-hold-first-ever-trilateral-dialogue/. Accessed on 13 June 2105.

Peri, Dinakar, 'IMAC will help Navy step up coastal surveillance'. *The Hindu*, 2014. Available at http://www.thehindu.com/news/national/imac-will-help-navy-step-up-coastal-surveillance/article6622612.ece. Accessed on 5 March 2015

Press Trust of India, 'Navy gets facility for uninterrupted communication with ships', 2014.

Mohan, C.R., 'Look East Policy - Phase Two', *The Hindu*, 9th October 2003.

Smith. M. Jeff., Andaman and Nicobar Islands: India's Strategic Outpost. *The Diplomat*, 2014. Available at http://thediplomat.com/2014/03/andaman-and-nicobar-islands-indias-strategic-outpost/. Accessed on 21 January 2015.

Standard Chartered Report, 2014. Available at https://research. standard chartered.com/configuration/ROW%20Documents/India_%E2%80%93_Unleashing_the_ASEAN_opportunity_21_08_14_05_39.pdf. Accessed on 3 May 2014.

World Economic Forum Report, 2013, Available at http://www3.weforum.org/docs/WEF_GlobalCompetitivenessReport_2012-13.pdf. Accessed on 13 August 2014

Index